It's the Little Things...

It's the Little Things...

An Appreciation
of Life's Simple Pleasures

Craig Wilson

Random House Trade Paperbacks

New York

A Random House Trade Paperback Original

Copyright © 2002 by Craig Wilson

All of the essays that appear in this work were originally
published in the *USA Today* newspaper column "The Final Word"
and are copyright © USA TODAY, a division of Gannett Co. Inc.

Grateful acknowledgment is made to Warner Bros. Publications Inc.
for permission to reprint an excerpt from "September Song" by Maxwell
Anderson and Kurt Weill. © 1938 (Renewed) Chappell & Co. and
TRO-Hampshire House Publishing Corp. All Rights Reserved. Used by
Permission. Warner Bros. Publications U.S. Inc., Miami, FL 33014.

Library of Congress Cataloging-in-Publication Data
Wilson, Craig.
It's the little things . . . : an appreciation of life's simple
pleasures / Craig Wilson.
p.   cm.
"Random House trade paperbacks"—T.p.
ISBN 0-375-75896-8
I. Title.
PN4874.W64 A25   2002   814'.6—dc21   2002021315

Random House website address: www.atrandom.com
Printed in the United States of America
246897531

TO JACK, MY ROCK

Acknowledgments

I would like to thank Tom Curley, publisher of *USA Today,* and my editors, who have made this all possible. I would also like to thank my mom, who gives me some of my best material.

Contents

Winter

Spring

Summer

Introduction

A Far Way from Home . . .

Some people are blessed with the best of both worlds. I'd like to think I might be one of them. I had the good fortune to grow up on a farm. I now live in the city. I have an edge over most people—I can walk between the two. I know the joys of sitting on the back of a farm wagon as it bounces down the dirt lane that cuts through the apple orchards. I also know the pleasure of a Sunday afternoon spent at an art gallery, soaking up the treasures the world has to offer.

I grew up on a fruit farm along Lake Ontario on the wind-swept plains of western New York. Orleans County. The Erie Canal cuts through its center; the world's largest apple pie was once baked at the county fair; and George Pullman, a local who gave the railroads the Pullman car, also gave the money for the church on Albion's courthouse square, where my parents were married in May of 1942. Times have changed. Once-elegant farms, their white barns gleaming in the summer sun, today sit abandoned, run-down, in need of love, attention, and a fresh coat of paint.

I now live in Georgetown, Washington, D.C.'s historic enclave of dinner parties and power salons, of polished brass door knockers behind which the cave dwellers dwell. I'm a far way from home.

Sally Quinn and Ben Bradlee live around the corner in the mansion that Abraham Lincoln's son once owned. They are big deals here on the D.C. A-list. Back home, few, if any, of the regulars at the Village Inn in Childs would know who they were. It is a thought that always makes me smile whenever I see them, which is not often. They rarely walk the streets with the neighbors.

When I go back home now to visit my mother, who still lives on the farm, I sometimes get the feeling some think of me as a city slicker. After almost twenty years here, they think I have crossed over to the other side. "Oh, you're a fancy city person now," one of my mother's friends said once . . . and she wasn't kidding. But I know what a fancy city person is, and I'm not one.

A couple of years ago, I attended a cocktail party at the late Katharine Graham's, then doyenne of Georgetown, owner of *The Washington Post*, lunch mate of Nancy Reagan, Pulitzer Prize winner. Her mansion, appropriately, sat on the top of the Georgetown hill. My town house sits at the bottom. But more than mere geography separated us. I was there only because of my job. She didn't know me from Adam, although when I thanked her for her hospitality as I was leaving, she said she was delighted I had come. She was hosting a book party for some author. I don't remember who now. But I do remember the waiters in white jackets coming around with glasses of wine on silver trays. I remember the Renoir hanging unassumingly in the corner of her front parlor. I remember the huge black-and-white photo of Princess Diana on the table in the library. I didn't do it that evening, but sometimes when I'm at a Georgetown cocktail party I will drop the fact that I grew up on a farm. To some I become a curiosity. One woman said she'd never met a farmer before and asked me if I could drive a tractor. I can. Another said I didn't sound as if I'd grown up on a farm. I wasn't sure what a person raised on a farm was supposed to sound like, so I asked her. "Oh, I don't know," she said, "but not like you." Others excuse themselves, scurrying away to the hors d'oeuvres. A farmer isn't of much use in Washington.

If I had stayed on the farm I would have been the fifth-generation Wilson to do so. But as lovely as the orchards are in bloom, and as wonderful as the harvest season is, I knew early on that that was not going to be my life. I didn't flee to the city immediately. I should have, but I wasn't that secure. I regret not going to New York City right out of college. I regret not sharing an apartment with a couple of guys, working some grunt job on Madison Avenue, embracing city life as only a twenty-one-year-old can. Instead I went to Saratoga Springs, which turned out to be my prep school, my holding tank for almost ten years. I was not yet ready for prime time. Saratoga had a fair amount of culture, Skidmore College, and a relatively educated populace, depending on the crowd you ran with. But it also had Zetterstrom's farm stand on the outskirts of town and enough front porches, enough barns, enough people who knew how to plant a proper garden, to make me feel at home.

When I left for Washington I was ready. I remember driving down Union Avenue, past the historic racetrack and Yaddo and out onto the Northway. I remember heading south, my freshly ironed shirts swaying on the pole that hung across the backseat. I also remember getting lost coming into Washington, seeing the Capitol dome off in the distance but never getting any closer to it the faster I drove. It was as if it were a mirage. Elusive. Unattainable. There are many who would say Washington is not the big time. I didn't know that then, but I would agree now. It is not New York or London or Paris. I thought I was moving to the big city where I could disappear into the crowd. Instead Washington turned out to be a small town, Georgetown an even smaller village within its boundaries. I left Saratoga Springs because I was tired of people knowing my every move. "Oh, I saw the Serlings were over to dinner Saturday night," a neighbor would say to me in the grocery store line on Monday. I quickly discovered that Scheele's Market, on the corner of Dumbarton and Twenty-ninth in Georgetown, is as much a center of gossip as Riemer's store was when I was growing up. The only difference is that Scheele's sells *Town & Country*, a nice French Chardonnay, and homemade baguettes. Reimer's sold the *Medina Daily Journal*, Genny Cream Ale, and Wonder Bread.

Not much separates country people from city people, really. Just subtleties. The type of wine you drink. The way you treat your dog. Front porches versus walled gardens. The pleasures of walking versus the necessity of driving. The process of picking out the Christmas tree.

Clotheslines.

Firewood.

Snowstorms.

They mean different things to different people. It just depends upon where you're standing—on the brick sidewalks of Georgetown or in a dusty orchard lane in upstate New York.

C.W.
Georgetown, Spring 2002

Fall

September

Oh, it's a long, long while
From May to December,
But the days grow short
When you reach September.
—"September Song"

Short, yes. But, oh, so sweet.

September, more than even those highly touted pastel months of spring, holds so much promise.

And more than even January, September heralds a new year. A new beginning.

New clothes.

New pencil boxes.

New friends.

Things start in September.

Things like school, with their floors all shiny and their books stacked high.

Pencils are long in September. Erasers full.

Everyone is an A student. Everyone is equal.

We're where we're supposed to be. Back home, and back to work. And we look good being there. We're rested. We still have that summer tan. But no longer do we have to worry about keeping to bathing suit weight. We pull on the corduroys, pull over that sweater, and cover up until spring.

We get new haircuts in September.

And haul out the stockings.

And put away the white shoes. We're sick of them anyway.

> Up from the meadows rich with corn,
> Clear in the cool September morn, . . .
>
> John Greenleaf Whittier

If you care about baseball, September brings the pennant races. If you're a Cleveland Indians fan, it means the pain is almost over.

"By then I've given up, and I've started following the [pro football] Browns," says Tom Wiener of Washington, D.C., an avid Indians fan, who has come to accept September's cruel fate. "That's the good thing about September. There's something new to move on to."

And if you don't care about football, you can wax your skis and not feel like a fool.

The first smell of rekindled fireplaces blankets the neighborhood. You see your breath for the first time in months.

You drink Scotch again.

Symphonies warm up.

The PTA comes back to life. School buses are everywhere.

> . . . Kids in slickers wait for buses; Sorry Sues and Gloomy Guses. Orchards swell with Red Delicious, Baldwins, Macs, and Northern Spies. Pickers work through rain like fishes, wiping their eyes.
>
> Tim Clark, *The Old Farmer's Almanac*

September has given us so many good things: the Constitution. Brigitte Bardot. Agatha Christie. George Gershwin.

The ice-cream cone was invented in September. A little late for that summer of 1903, but better late than never.

And Labor Day is always in September. You have to love a month that has a holiday named Labor when no one works.

September also has the honor of always ushering in autumn. This year: 7:48 A.M. EST on the twenty-third.

> Fall, leaves, fall; die, flowers, away;
> Lengthen night and shorten day; . . .
>
> Emily Brontë

June's a cliché. We march down the aisle in September now.

"The weather is better, and everyone is back," says Hedda Kleinfeld, of Kleinfeld's bridal salon in Brooklyn, New York. She dressed over a thousand brides for this September.

"September is really the beginning of the year, and for the bride, your choices for dresses are wonderful," she says. "You can wear what you wish. You don't have to do summer or winter. You can have a satin dress if you want."

The world is heady with harvest. Apples in Washington State. Cranberries on Cape Cod. Mums everywhere.

"September's that wonderful lull between the music season in August and the ski season," says Aspen, Colorado, restaurateur Lauretta Bonfiglio. "September's the time for the local people to enjoy. It's the mellow time. And the most beautiful time."

Miss America gets her crown in September.

The Atlantic loses its warmth.

So does the sun.

See you in September . . .

September is the time of reunions.

You return to college. To old haunts and old friends and old habits, good and bad.

Every club from the Lions to the Elks congregates then. If there's something to sign up for, we sign up for it in September.

It's a good month to fall in love, too. The slate is often clean. The summer romance is over. He's gone back from where he came. So has she.

"September offers some kind of hope," says Cheryl Lavin, whose syndicated romance and relationship advice column, "Tales from the Front," appears in more than fifty newspapers. "But you have to be careful in September. We get letters from women who sign up for fall night courses, say, in the stock market, and walk in and find thirty other women."

Okay, so September has a few things going against it. The new TV season starts. It will bomb before October. And Congress returns to its shenanigans. Halloween candy is already lurking at the drugstore, and Christmas wrapping looms.

But babies galore are born in September, conveniently placed nine months after the season of good cheer. This September we find out if our favorite TV news queen, Murphy Brown, will have a child of her own.

The weather's nice almost everywhere, except for the hurricanes brewing in the Caribbean. But we're not in the Caribbean. We're home. Remember?

Lavin, for instance, always stays in Chicago in September.

"It's that time between too hot and too cold," she says. "You don't want to leave town and miss it. It's the one time of year you might get a couple of days of good weather."

But if you can, September remains the best time to vacation. Weather's still lovely. The beaches and mountains are empty. And prices fall with the evening temperatures.

Linda Bucci, an elementary school teacher in Ballston Spa, New York, can't take a September vacation. It doesn't matter.

"For me, it's a rebirth because my year isn't January to January, it's September to September," she says. "And there's that scent in the air. You walk out in the morning and it's cool and crisp and in the afternoon it's warm and sunny. You can feel winter's coming, but that's okay in September."

My First-Grade Teacher

Her name was Miss Meinke. Or maybe it was Menke.

What did I know? I was in first grade and she was my teacher. I couldn't even spell my own name at the time, let alone hers.

It didn't matter. I was going to marry her and change her name to mine and that would take care of that problem once and for all.

I loved her. And I know she loved me. It was obvious, just by the way she winked at me when I came in the room.

She was kind and good and noble—all the things a first-time love should be. She never shouted, never scolded. She praised my every move.

For hours we'd push mahogany-colored chestnuts back and forth across the table. She called it a counting exercise, but I knew it was more than that.

I remember she was tall and willowy. Maybe she was short and dumpy, but in 1954, when I was three feet high, she was tall and willowy. And she had a long and beautiful neck, the way ballerinas' are.

She smelled good, too. Nothing racy. Not Miss Meinke. She wasn't that kind of girl.

I was by no means the first student to fall in love with his teacher, and I certainly wasn't going to be the last.

This fall millions of kids will have crushes on their own Miss Meinkes, staying late for special help they don't need, asking questions they already know the answers to. Some will even offer up the proverbial shiny apple to the newest woman in their lives. Could her first name be Eve?

I didn't know Miss Meinke's first name. First-grade teachers didn't have first names back then. Nor did they have personal lives.

I remember seeing her at the supermarket once and thinking how odd that was. She buys food? She cooks? She eats at places other than the teachers' table in the cafeteria?

To me she lived only in that crowded and cluttered pastel-colored classroom. Maybe she slept under her desk. I never asked. But I would be the one to take her away from all that. Who cared if there was a thirty-year age difference? Not me. Why wouldn't she want a younger man? Someone to look after her later on.

It was a perfect match.

There's a book out this fall on the subject of student/teacher infatuation, but I don't think it discusses puppy love.

It's titled *The Erotics of Instruction.* A rather buxom young coed graces the cover. She's smiling, perhaps because she's in love with her freshman English professor and can't wait to get to his class. She even has a pencil in her hand, ready to take down his every word.

But freshman English professors are not first-grade teachers. On the college level it's not the way it is in first grade. These guys have been around the quad a few times. Not Miss Meinke.

In college it's about the lure of older men in tweed jackets, about the aphrodisiac of pseudointellectualism, about the smell of a professor's smoldering pipe filling a cluttered office. Rumor is, it might even involve sex.

Miss Meinke never had sex. She was pure and innocent and saving herself for me.

We've all heard stories about professors writing sonnets to adoring nubile coeds. Miss Meinke never wrote me a sonnet. I understand now that she really couldn't, seeing that everything I took home I immediately showed to my mother. So she did the only thing she could. She sent messages on my report card.

The first came in October. On it she wrote that basically I was the ideal young man. "A delight to have in my classroom" were her exact words. I still have the card. Now, if that wasn't a thinly veiled "I'm in love with Craig!" I don't know what was.

But it wasn't meant to be.

She left me. For another man, I found out later. Out in California. She left upstate New York the next fall and never looked back. Never wrote. Never called.

In retrospect I understand it was her way of coping. What else could she do? I had already moved on to an older, more mature woman, Mrs. Bane, who lived down the hall in a place called second grade.

The School Bus

I didn't walk three miles through the snow to school, as my father says he did.

Instead, for thirteen years, I rode a bus. Ten miles into town. Ten miles home.

I would say it's a toss-up as to who had it worse. I would have preferred the walk in the snow.

Riding a school bus is probably the best training for what life will throw at you later—the bumps, the noise, the waiting, the sweaty masses, the cold drafts, the feeling that you're moving along but getting nowhere.

I remember thinking it was kind of exciting when I first boarded in kindergarten, this big yellow machine stopping at the end of the driveway to take me miles from home.

I pulled myself up those stairs that seemed made for Wilt Chamberlain, found myself a seat—lots were already "saved" for the in crowd who got on after me—and looked out over the countryside from my elevated perch. I felt a bit like James Cameron. King of the world. Or of my world, at least.

But the novelty wore off quickly, and the next dozen years riding bus No. 12 were a mixture of dread and resignation.

The seats were hard, the windows leaked, the heating system sputtered, and there was no suspension to speak of.

Whatever we rode over we felt, right to the seat of our corduroy pants. The bumps that amused us in second grade had long since lost their thrill by junior high.

And then there was the kid who never seemed to get the hang of the bus-riding thing, throwing up at least once a week when his stomach deemed the journey too jostling. If nothing else, he was reliable.

The fact that I rode the bus all the way to the end of my high school career is embarrassing, of course, because by the time you're a senior, you're way too sophisticated to ride the bus. When you're a senior in high school, you're way too sophisticated to even *be* in high school.

But my parents refused to drive me to school on the grounds that a forty-five-minute bus ride was good for my character.

I didn't have a car of my own, and I didn't have any friends who had cars, either. It's an odd concept to grasp today, but most high school kids didn't have cars then. So there I was, relegated to the status of bus nerd by the randomness of being born a farm boy.

There was no disputing the caste system. Those who had cars were on top, the walkers who lived in town were next, and then came us, the bus riders, the bottom of the heap. My brother, who would do almost anything *not* to ride the bus, made friends with car people. He was shameless about it. He and his "friends" would ceremoniously pass the bus on the way home, waving and laughing at us losers as they sped away down the road.

Bill Whitney, my bus driver for most of those years, never seemed a very happy man. I now understand why he sometimes brandished a paddle.

Think about it. He not only had to drive one of the most

awkward machines ever made, he had to do it with sixty children screaming in his ear, and often in a snowstorm. It's no wonder he was always scowling at us through the huge rearview mirror that hung above his head.

Not that I was ever one of those screaming kids, although I do remember he pulled the bus over to the side of the road once, came back down the aisle, grabbed my genuine simulated rawhide book binder right out of my hand, and hit me over the head with it. Needless to say, I was stunned.

I'm sure I deserved it, but for the life of me I can't remember what I could have been doing to deserve such public punishment. It calmed me down for the rest of the trip home, but I remember thinking that that Donna girl who lived down the road, the one who always smacked everyone with her lunch box, was getting away with murder.

The *really* bad kids, of course, sat way in the back of the bus, where they yelled out things to intimidate those of us seated in front of them. It worked.

I never went back there, but I always had a view of what was going on because one of the rules of riding a school bus is that you never sit facing forward. You always face backward, talking to your friends over the seat while surveying the scene, which included whatever was happening in the backseat, which more often than not was quite a bit.

Once, the hoods—they were called hoods in those days—were necking in the backseat, and we all watched until the boy hood told us to turn around or he'd beat us up. We all spun around so fast, I swear the bus swerved.

We may have been bus nerds, but we weren't fools.

The First Day of College

I remember the day as if it were yesterday. It was one of those glorious early September days in upstate New York, when it's still sunny and clear and the sky is a brilliant blue, but there's something in the air that tells you autumn is not far away.

It was the day my parents took me to college, and it was one of the happiest days of my life. It was also one of the saddest. I've never been divorced, but I think there are certain similarities.

We drove the three hours to college, the trunk of my dad's car filled with clothes I would not wear once I got there. While it was still the era of preppy back-to-campus clothes—crewneck sweaters, Bass Weejuns—it soon became the era of bell-bottoms and tie-dyed T-shirts. The transition happened overnight my freshman year, 1967.

Also making the journey was a stereo (with detachable speakers!), a desk lamp, a blotter, a brand-new dictionary, and a corduroy bedspread that matched a corduroy pillow with arms my mother thought would be good back support when I sat on my bed and studied. Her heart was in the right place.

I remember the chaos when we pulled in front of the dorm. Cars were lined up for what seemed like miles, and upperclassmen were scurrying around, helping the freshmen move in. It was a Syracuse tradition. I would do it the following fall. They were carrying everything from luggage to lamps, stereos to surfboards. I don't have a clue what someone does with a surfboard in central New York, but there it was.

Before I knew it, all my worldly possessions were piled on the dorm room floor, and my mother began making the twin bed with the sheets we'd brought from home. They matched the bedspread and pillow. Pale orange.

I remember being overwhelmed and exhilarated. There I was, seventeen, about to embark on an amazing adventure. I was thrilled and scared and maybe a little bit homesick, even though I had left home but a few hours before.

The experience was made harder because I actually liked my parents. We got along. For three years, I was an only child after my brother went to college.

That is not to say I wanted to live with them the rest of my life. I wasn't that big a nerd. And, of course, they embarrassed me, as all parents are supposed to do. But they were good company, and I didn't mind going out with them on a Friday night for a fish fry, something my older brother would never have been caught dead doing, even if he had nothing else to do.

My parents hung around for a while. We went to a place off campus for lunch, where I remember we sat for the most part in silence. They asked if I needed to go to the bookstore to buy anything we might have forgotten. I said I didn't. They were stalling.

When the car finally pulled up in front of the dorm, I quickly kissed them good-bye, jumped out, and walked away, never looking back.

Did they sit there and watch me walk out of their daily lives? Or did they pull away immediately? I never knew.

I went up to my room and sat on the corduroy-covered bed my mother had just made. And yes, I cried.

My Freshman Floor

My nephew Ben is off at college. Freshman year.

Knowing how busy college freshmen are, with their studies and all, I'm a bit surprised he had time to write. But he did. A quick e-mail.

"My roommate is cool. His name is Pete. I don't see him a whole lot, but we get along great. We play video games with the guys next door. That accounts for most of my sleep deprivation."

We didn't know of video games at Syracuse University back in September of '67.

We did know of sleep deprivation, however.

My first morning as a college freshman, I was awakened by my roommate putting on his shoes. His method amounted to kicking the toes of his Bass Weejuns against the wall. It took longer than one might think. It became my daily reveille.

At night, I was kept awake by his blowing on a stack of pennies he would arrange on the edge of his desk. He liked to see how far back he could stand and still topple them. It was far. I don't have a clue what was going on there, but I quickly learned the fine art of living with someone you do not love.

In truth, he wasn't a bad guy. He took his pennies and battered loafers and transferred to Cornell at the end of the year.

I never saw him again, though I've often wondered about the state of his toes.

My freshman floor in Booth Hall was, as all freshman floors are, where my college education began. Forget freshman English. It was on Booth 7 that I learned the important lessons of life.

I learned that a rum and Coke does not mix with peanuts, that projectile vomiting is different from run-of-the-mill vomiting, that you can make a fool of yourself faster than you ever thought.

I learned how long you can go without doing laundry. Chuck, across the hall, went a full semester. I also learned that my mother's sewing my name on all my clothing was an act of both love and futility.

I learned that all-night pinochle games lead to academic probation, that a care package from home was to be guarded with your life, and that it's possible to inhale a huge square of Jell-O in one fell swoop.

John, who lived down the hall and is now a college professor, performed this feat in the dining hall nightly, to the amazement of all. (Do not try this with fruit in the Jell-O.)

And in no time I also learned the caste system of eighteen-year-old college freshmen.

Cool jocks.

Cool jerks.

The rest of us.

Lacrosse players, gods at Syracuse, would practice their passing techniques nightly in the hall, their sticks whipping that hard little ball back and forth at amazing speeds. I know. I stopped one once with my head.

I also learned that the cool crowd came from Great Neck

and Chicago, not the farms of upstate New York. They wore shag haircuts, form-fitting bell-bottoms, Canoe.

They drank Mateus.

One of the cool crowd also was named Craig. He was from Chicago and wore ski boots around the dorm in October— "I'm breaking them in for Colorado." He also wore sunglasses in February. Inside. At night.

He had as many phone calls as he had girlfriends.

"Craig! Phone!" echoed up and down the cinder-block hall a dozen times a night my freshman year.

It was then, very early on, that I learned probably life's most important lesson: It's not always for you.

Thanksgiving Antipasto

Thanksgiving used to be so simple. A Butterball turkey, some mashed potatoes with gravy, frozen peas from the bag, and an apple pie with cheese on the side. Nothing exotic. Traditions were kept.

Everyone went home happy.

But our Thanksgiving gathering has grown so large this year that auxiliary plans have had to be implemented. For one, the location has been moved to my friend Susan's more spacious home. For another, the increased crowd size warranted an actual meeting where who's-going-to-bring-what was the topic of discussion. It began with wine, as all such meetings must. It also ended with wine.

Not being the cook in this crowd of cooks, I was immediately relegated to the one-man decorating committee, meaning I have to come up with three centerpieces by tomorrow because there are going to be three tables of six this year. I can only assume they had heard I was decorating chairman of my high school prom—themed "Hawaiian Sunset"—which folks in upstate New York are still talking about.

And then I was ignored, as was Rick, who was elected bartender. Our jobs, for the evening, were over. We sat against the wall. The discussion began.

My partner, Jack, brought out a long list of culinary possibilities, including three recipes for sweet potatoes. Seemed a bit excessive to me, but I said nothing.

The committee voted, accepting two of his recipes, including the one that calls for Southern Comfort, and that was that. Someone then declared that with two sweet potato dishes, we didn't need mashed potatoes this year. Not believing my ears, I could no longer remain a casual observer.

"Are you trying to kill my eighty-two-year-old mother?" I asked. "She's not coming all the way from New York to not have mashed potatoes for Thanksgiving. Where would her gravy go?"

Realizing that I meant business, the committee added mashed potatoes to the list. And gravy, of course.

Our friend Caroline began her presentation by saying that her father, who also was traveling from New York for the holiday, would require his annual creamed onions. They needed to be in the mix. There could be no discussion. I understood completely.

Creamed onions were quietly added to the list, along with Ocean Spray cranberry jelly from a can, another Scullin family tradition.

The newest member of our group, Patti, then announced she could bring antipasto, although she didn't call it antipasto. Being a true Italian American from New York, she just said *antipast*.

There was silence.

Never in Jack's fifty-four years has he had an "antipast" as a Thanksgiving hors d'oeuvre. And he was not alone. Nowhere in my fifty-two years, or Caroline's forty-two, or Susan's fifty-something years had such a platter appeared before the turkey. Rick admitted he'd never seen such a thing either—that was, until he married Patti.

But I'm happy to report that in the post–September 11 spirit of inclusion and expansiveness and ecumenicalism and kindness, the *antipast* was voted in.

I'm telling my mother it's a relish tray.

The Butterball

Year after year there are troublemakers out there who try to tart up the Thanksgiving feast. Mostly those foodies from New York City.

Fools. Every last one of them.

Any American worth his Jell-O mold knows that any dish that calls for veal kidneys or two codfish heads or clarified butter does not belong at the Thanksgiving table. Whatever clarified butter is.

We all know this is the time for gelatin salad rings, green beans covered with Campbell's cream of mushroom soup, and not to be forgotten, that old warhorse, the venerable frozen pea. Add those black olives, pickles, and carrots on a pressed-glass relish tray, and you've got yourself a feast.

Everyone I know has a family favorite that has graced the Thanksgiving table as long as they can remember. This dish *must* be served at Thanksgiving or the world will end. We're talking tradition here, not culinary excellence.

My family has a must-have-or-it's-not-Thanksgiving dish. It's my Grandmother Wilson's lime-green Jell-O salad with grapefruit floating in it. And it must be in the shape of a ring. No leaping-fish mold for us. Methodists appreciate the beauty of a simple circle.

I remember being impressed how Grandma always succeeded in making the grapefruit sections float. Not a one sank to the bottom, which of course was the top when she flipped the thing over onto a carefully made bed of lettuce.

My cousin Martha has kept the tradition alive, right down to the bowl of Hellmann's mayonnaise that sits in the center. As you can see, my family clings to the elegance of yesteryear.

Presentation is important at Thanksgiving. My co-worker Mary says her family's tradition is the cranberry jelly that comes from a can. Her mom just plops it out, still in the shape of the can, but puts it on a "very, very nice dish," which dresses it up nicely.

Perhaps the all-time, all-Thanksgiving favorite is sweet potatoes with marshmallows. Now, I'm not talking my family here. My family wouldn't be caught dead with a marshmallow anywhere on the Thanksgiving table, but my friend Katy says it wouldn't be Thanksgiving at her mom's house without a nice layer of those tiny marshmallows melted over the sweet potatoes. She grows misty-eyed just talking about it.

Stop snickering. The holidays are no time for food snobbery.

Now let's get back to the green beans for a minute, the ones with the Campbell's mushroom soup poured over them. We're not done discussing them. I left out the fact that on special occasions, like Thanksgiving, the dish is often topped with those onion rings from a can. Durkee, I believe, but I don't know why I know that.

Again, my family never did this, but to millions you might as well not have a turkey if you don't have this casserole on the table.

Which brings me to my father.

He was a practical man who loved his Butterball turkey.

Year after year after year, even though we lived in the country and not far from a turkey farm, he'd go to the grocery store in town and buy a frozen Butterball turkey. Hard as a rock. It took days to thaw it out in the kitchen sink. (I know, I know. This shouldn't be done, but I'm still here to talk about it, so how bad could it be? Besides, parents are never wrong.)

To us, it was the most American thing we could eat.

A few years ago he came to my house for Thanksgiving, and in a moment of complete lunacy, I went to one of those fancy gourmet shops and ordered a fresh turkey.

The day before Thanksgiving I picked it up, brought it home, cooked it to a luscious shade of brown, and served it up with a grand flourish.

My father took one look.

"This isn't a Butterball, is it?" he asked.

Right then and there I knew my feast was a failure.

I had strayed.

It wouldn't happen again.

Mom's Gravy

I live in a small house with an even smaller kitchen. There are no expansive granite counters in my life. It's comfortable for one cook, cozy with two, cramped with three.

I have long subscribed to the mantra that too many cooks spoil the broth, so I'm always happy to let my partner, Jack, have the run of the place. But on Thanksgiving, I have no choice. Neither does my mother, who is also allergic to kitchens.

It's usually about three in the afternoon, half an hour before we all sit down for Thanksgiving dinner, when we three cooks converge for our annual banging of the Calphalon.

Jack mashes the potatoes under the watchful eye of my mother, who every year issues the same edict: "Don't whip them as much as you did last year!"

Mom makes the gravy, which I have to admit she's very good at. With a martini in one hand and a metal whisk in the other, she stirs and stirs and stirs the drippings and flour and potato water in the roasting pan.

And every year, without fail, when Jack announces we're only minutes away from calling everyone to the table, she says the gravy isn't anywhere near ready. Not even close.

This never pleases Jack. As crowded a kitchen as ours is, there's always room for a little tension.

Meanwhile, I'm in the corner, carving the turkey. No one bothers me because no one knows how to carve a turkey. Dad took that skill with him to the grave, so I'm left alone to hack away. And hack away I do.

As you can see, we have this all worked out—a fine-tuned kitchen humming along like any five-star restaurant. Not that things can't fall apart.

Just as we were doing our thing a couple of years ago, a terrible clatter came from the dining room.

When I looked, Murphy, our dog, was covered in Grandma Wilson's famous fruit salad, which had been sitting on the sideboard—that was until Murphy decided she wanted a taste and flipped the bowl with her paw.

Fruit salad was everywhere. Murphy was licking whipped cream and mandarin oranges off her beard.

I took the bowl into the kitchen to recover what I could (guests don't need to know what's happening behind the scenes), chose another bowl, and was about to transfer what was left of the salad, when my mother said what only a mother could say at a time like this.

"Oh, you're not going to use *that* bowl, are you?"

I snapped. I used a word I had never used in front of my mother. I used it as an adjective. I told her if she was so unhappy with my selection, she could find her own, well, bowl.

I couldn't believe what had come out of my mouth. I froze, waiting for the inevitable "Craig Wilson! I didn't bring you up to talk like that!"

Her reaction was exactly the opposite. Mom started hopping up and down, crossed her legs, and laughed so hard that gin spilled into the roasting pan.

Best Thanksgiving gravy we ever had.

The Kids' Table

I did not grow up in a large family, but when I was a kid it was large enough that we all couldn't fit around the Thanksgiving table.

So, being the youngest, I was relegated to the children's table, along with my brother and my cousin, who were no happier being there with me than I was with them. They kicked.

My mother told me it was a special table, but I knew she was lying. If it was so special, she would have sat there. She didn't.

I hated it, being stuck over in the corner of the dining room next to the radiator.

I should have known I was going to grow up to work at a newspaper. Even back then I needed to know what was going on, and what was going on was at the big table, not at the kids' table.

The chatter sounded so important, so interesting, so grown-up. If my brother and cousin were talking about anything at our table, it was what they were going to do to me next. At the big table, meantime, the world's problems were being solved.

So there I sat, looking at my aunt's back, hoping that someday I would graduate to the better dishes, the better conversation, the better location. As they say, location is everything, and for some reason I knew that at a very young age.

And then it happened. Aunt Edith had to die to clear the way, but there I was one Thanksgiving afternoon sitting with the big boys. The view was spectacular. I saw gravy boats sailing on a sea of white linen. I saw flickering candles and butter on ice. I saw mountains of mashed potatoes in china bowls, and they were beautiful. So this is what being a grown-up is all about, I told myself. I had finally arrived.

And what a letdown it was.

How could the conversation that seemed so fascinating just a year before turn so deadly upon my arrival?

But there they all were, talking about God knows what. The apple crop, Howard Miller's new snowplow attachment for his garden tractor, the new minister at church, whom no one was quite sure about yet. He drove a Buick, a little too flashy for a Methodist.

All I remember is thinking I had waited a long time to get to this spot, only to find out the journey was for naught.

I stayed at the grown-up table for years. It got no better, not that I didn't try to help things along. When I was in college, when I knew most everything there was to know and was very happy to share my knowledge, I even introduced new topics to the mix. God knows I was trying.

My favorite Thanksgiving conversation at the time was the Vietnam War. My family did not share my enthusiasm for the topic. The fact that they didn't share my views didn't help, either.

It became clear very quickly that polite conversation was not only appreciated, but expected at the Thanksgiving table. We ate our peas and minded our q's.

I finally resigned myself to the fact that Thanksgiving meant my grandmother's great lime Jell-O ring with grapefruit sections floating in it, not salon conversation with the likes of Clare Boothe Luce or Gertrude Stein.

Then, a few years ago, the tables turned again. Cousins married and had children, and we were once again setting up a children's table over in the corner by the radiator.

But it was in my dining room this time, and being the host of the family Thanksgiving dinner now, I volunteered to be at the kids' table again.

To be honest, I like it there. It doesn't seem so bad this time around, and I certainly don't worry about what's being said at the grown-up table anymore. Been there. Heard that.

This is not to say the conversation with my young dinner partners runs to Kierkegaard. It doesn't. Barney and bathroom humor are more like it, but hey, it's lively, full of surprises, and moves along at a quick pace. There's also some showing of chewed food, which adds a certain drama to the dining experience, something sorely lacking at the big table.

My young relatives sharing the table with me aren't abandoning me yet. They're still too young to be vying for a seat with the grown-ups. That will come in a few years, when they start believing, as I once did, that bigger is better.

As for me, I'm staying put.

At my age, I know there are much worse corners of the world than those with a little table next to a warm radiator.

And at my kids' table, we serve a lovely little Merlot.

Old Family Photos

Like most first apartments, mine was furnished with hand-me-downs from home. The peg-legged sofa, the matching chair, the kitchen table all came from either my parents' basement or my grandmother's attic.

Early eclectic. *House Beautiful* it was not.

Among this hodgepodge of tall lamps and low end tables was a large photograph of a woman, an ancestor perhaps, although no one in my immediate family knew who she was or where she had come from. She was in a rather lovely gold frame, however, and since I had nothing but ski posters to tack to the wall, I took her with me and hung her over the fireplace.

She was a stern-looking woman of indeterminate age, her hair pulled back in a bun, but there was something about her stare that said she had a story to tell.

For lack of a better name, I called her Ida, and not a day passed that I didn't look at her and ask who she was.

Finally, when my interior design budget increased, I removed her from her prominent position and put her in the closet, her story still untold.

In truth, I put her away because she was making me melancholy. Old photographs have that effect on me.

Not old photos of people I know something about—like my ancestors in the Wilson and Weaver clans. I know them, their names, the stories of their lives. I know who married, who didn't, who died early, who lived into their nineties, and who was a character, like my Great-grandmother Weaver. Known for her henna wigs and sassy tongue, she died watching wrestling on her rabbit-eared TV. I can look at photos of her for hours.

It's the faces of the abandoned, staring out from brown and faded photographs, that make me sad.

I was in an antique shop in rural Indiana the other day, looking for nothing in particular, when I came upon a box of old photographs, priced to sell. I sat down to thumb through the pile and ended up doing what I always do—studying their faces, asking them to tell me their stories.

There was a row of turn-of-the-century dandies in pleated pants and bow ties. One of them, the biggest one with the grandest mustache, appeared to be the ringleader, rallying his troops.

Someone's son, now lost.

There were women in white dresses and big hats, sitting under an arbor long since gone. Were they reading sonnets? One of them had a book in her lap. Or perhaps the conversation was a bit racier. It's their secret now.

Someone's daughters, now forgotten.

There were boys with their horses, men with their dogs, and dozens of photos of women in solitary poses. Like Ida, still keeping their own counsel.

But through their silent stares, they speak volumes. "I was here!" I hear them saying. "I have a story to tell!"

They had husbands and wives, brothers and sisters, dreams and disappointments. They went to work, and they went to war. And they should be home with their families now, in frames and albums on a living room shelf.

They deserve better than a cardboard box and a stranger's glance, their lives worth more than fifty cents a frame.

Thanksgiving *Feng Shui*

For decades, I lived a perfectly nice life, never paying much attention to the placement of my sofa in the den or my guests at the dining room table.

Then along came the *feng shui* craze, that ancient Eastern practice of marshaling energy. The belief is that where you place things can make a difference in the quality of your life.

Suddenly, people all over America were rearranging their furniture. I had a friend who kept moving her bed around in an effort to capture just the right energy (i.e., boyfriend). It didn't work.

I'm not one for change. I've lived in the same house for fifteen years, and for those fifteen years my dining room table has been in the same place, under a small brass chandelier in the center of the room.

Call me madcap, but it works for me.

And for fifteen years, whenever I've hosted a dinner party or Thanksgiving dinner, I've always sat in the same place—the north end of the table, facing south. My partner, Jack, is at the other end, facing me. Our guests are along the sides, facing east and west.

So far no one has died, fallen in the mashed potatoes, or

left in a huff, so I have considered these dinners a success. I daresay some guests have even left having had a good time.

Now I learn I've been lucky.

Very lucky.

According to yet another *feng shui* book, where you sit at a table not only dictates how you're going to act, but also comes with dangers. (This book also says that what you eat can actually affect how you feel. Imagine that.)

"Think carefully about your seating plan, as the direction you face when you eat will have a tremendous impact on how you respond to the food, the atmosphere and to those around you," warn the authors of *Feng Shui Food*, two guys who obviously have been to far too many bad dinner parties.

Next to this warning is an illustration of people seated at a table. There I was, in the north seat, facing south. And next to my chair, the authors noted my position's strengths and weaknesses: Helpful "for expression and excitement"; dangers were "becoming proud and over-emotional."

Me?

Overemotional at a dinner party?

I quickly looked to see what was written next to Jack's chair.

His position was helpful "for feeling introspective and calm"; the danger was being "uncommunicative."

I confess: He has complained more than once that he can never get a word in edgewise.

Other chairs around the table came with *feng shui* warnings, too. The guest in the middle on my right, the one facing east, will most likely be self-confident and enthusiastic but could become impatient.

My mother sits there every Thanksgiving.

And the west-facing guest opposite her most likely will become overindulgent.

Our neighbor Caroline often sits there.

And so it went around the table. The clingy guest, the self-righteous guest, the thoughtless guest.

I'm thinking of moving everyone to different chairs this Thanksgiving. Just for fun. Then again, maybe not.

My friend Deirdre tells me one shouldn't mess with the *feng shui* gods.

Besides, I can deal with an impatient mother. An overemotional one, trying to make gravy, is the last thing we need on a Thanksgiving afternoon.

Firewood

Some people look forward to the first robin. Others can't wait for the beach to open.

My favorite season arrives when Junior Bowers comes down the street in his old pickup truck loaded with firewood.

Junior is from Culpeper, Virginia, and has a rural Shenandoah Valley accent thick enough to confuse any transplanted Yankee, which is what I am, and which is what he does.

When I first opened my door to him more than a dozen years ago, he said only one word.

"Furwood?" I didn't have a clue what he was saying.

"Pardon?" I asked.

"Furwood!" he repeated. "Do you need any *furwood?"*

"Oh, firewood," I replied after looking past him and eyeing his truck. "Yes. Yes. I want firewood."

Little did Junior Bowers know that that was his lucky day. He was to become my lifetime supplier.

I bought a cord of wood from Junior that early autumn day. I never asked the price. Price didn't matter. To me it's priceless.

There's something about firewood that stirs my soul. I'm

sure there are some who feel the same about canning tomatoes, but for me it's firewood. Nothing makes me happier.

Maybe I was a squirrel in a former life. Maybe it's the gathering of supplies for the long winter months that gives me such a warm feeling inside.

All I know is that firewood makes me feel secure, prepared, ready for whatever the coming months might bring.

The ozone layer could evaporate; the stock market could crash; the Yankees could lose (and did!). It doesn't matter.

We have wood. Nothing bad can happen to us now.

Or maybe it's my anal retentiveness, my futile attempts to bring order to a chaotic world. Who knows? All I know is there's no more beautiful sight than firewood stacked in long, perfect rows. Sculpture at its most honest.

Junior came by the other day and now, once again, outside my dining room door, stands a five-foot-tall wall of firewood. I catch myself standing there staring at it.

It's not just my firewood either that makes me happy. I can get a rush from anyone's wood stack. They all have the same effect on me.

I went to a friend's weekend cabin in West Virginia a few years ago, and there on the ground was a huge pile of firewood. It was haunting her, she said, just sitting there demanding to be stacked under her deck before the winter snows blew down the valley.

Little did she know she had given me one of the best weekends of my life. While the rest of the guests relaxed, took long walks and naps, I stacked firewood. For hours. Later she said it was as if I were on a drug.

I was.

Could I live without it? I can and I have, but I can't do it for long periods of time.

Once I lived in an apartment where the landlord allowed the tenants to burn only those fake logs you buy at the supermarket checkout line. We all know those logs are no more firewood than Madonna is Marilyn Monroe.

I tried to break the lease after I was told of the clause, but it was too late. What was the point? I asked her. A fireplace with no firewood.

I suffered firewood envy that year. Friends had beautiful rows of firewood proudly lining their porches.

Me? I had a box of chemical logs hiding in the closet. I never burned them in front of anyone. It was too embarrassing. In fact I rarely burned them for myself. I think half the box was still left when spring arrived. They went out with the trash.

But no more. Now I have Junior Bowers. Now I have *furwood.*

Furwood. What a beautiful word.

I was telling a colleague the other day that I couldn't imagine living anywhere where there was no change of seasons. Where there was no putting away the shorts, no pulling out the sweaters, no stacking the firewood at the back door in anticipation of what winter might throw our way.

She didn't get it.

She had just moved east from Los Angeles and didn't know the joys of a good down parka, let alone the beauty to be found in a stack of firewood. It was all a mystery to her. She was polite, but in truth I knew she thought I was a nutcase.

She then said the unthinkable. She said that fall made her depressed (it was the harbinger of winter), and that having the same weather all the time was really quite wonderful.

"You get used to it," she said. "We'd still change clothes,

no matter what the weather. We'd still put on corduroys and sweaters in the fall. We'd just sort of pretend."

It was then I knew she *really* didn't get it.

Firewood isn't pretend.

Ironing

Years ago, when I was about to go off to college, my mom decided it was time I learned to iron a shirt.

She set the ironing board up in the kitchen, plugged in the iron, pulled a shirt out of the laundry basket, and turned it over.

She began by ironing the back of the collar.

"That way you can tell if the iron's too hot," she said. "If it is and you scorch the shirt a little, you really haven't done any damage."

She was wrong. Even starting under the collar, I scorched a dryerful of shirts in the beginning. But before the end of my first semester I got the hang of it, and if I do say so myself, went on to become a world-class ironer.

Odder still, I enjoyed it. Still do.

Bring me your tired, your crumpled, your wrinkled, yearning to be creased. I will oblige.

I'm an anachronism, I know. No one irons anymore unless they're paid to, although I suspect there are more than a few closet ironers out there who on occasion enjoy whipping an oxford-cloth shirt into shape.

My friend Ann said that the last time she ironed anything was in high school. For her sake we won't say how long ago that was. Let's just say a lot of spray starch has left the can between then and now.

Not me. I iron every week. Usually Sunday afternoons. This has earned me the title of neighborhood nutcase.

I almost always iron to the soundtrack from *The Big Chill*, so when Marvin Gaye starts belting out "I Heard It Through the Grapevine," my next-door neighbor Nancy amuses herself by watching me through the kitchen window as I sing and spray. She needs to get a life, but you can see that.

"I can't believe you iron," she still says after four years of Sunday afternoons. "It's just too strange."

Old friends are much more understanding about my ironing fetish. The damp, rolled-up shirts in the refrigerator, the ones tucked between the lettuce and the Parmesan, are no longer a surprise to them when they come to visit. (For ironing virgins, cool damp shirts iron much better than bone-dry ones.)

I'm secure about my ironing now, but it wasn't always that way. In college, the other guys used to talk about me in whispers.

"Yeah, the guy in 703 *irons*," they'd say. "Too weird."

But they stopped snickering when they needed a shirt for a special occasion. Like going out in public.

They would knock on my door with a sheepish look on their face and a crumpled shirt in their hand, asking if I could just touch it up a little bit.

I remember one guy told me the "touch-up" was for his grandmother's funeral. His grandmother died about ten times that semester.

During those college years, I fear, I ironed more dirty shirts than clean ones, but my theory was an ironed dirty shirt was better than a wrinkled dirty shirt. It was my small contribution to a more aesthetically pleasing society. Considering it was the late sixties, I was definitely ironing upstream.

My love of ironing has to do with my need for order, of course. I know this. But early on, I found it actually therapeutic. Unlike a lot of chores, you can see where you've been. Kind of like plowing a field. There's a sense of accomplishment.

There you are, a pile of clothes on the chair staring at you like a dog in need of a good brushing, and when you're done, the shirts are hanging in a row from the kitchen cupboard, pressed, crisp, a sight to behold. There's no prettier thing than a perfect crease going down the length of a sleeve.

But enough rhapsodizing.

The good news is that ironing is so out that it might be on its way back in.

Martha Stewart, who's making millions recycling everything our grandmothers knew instinctively years ago, has a primer in her newest issue. It's called "Ironing a Shirt."

It begins with this bit of advice: The ironing board must never be wobbly.

How did we ever get along without her?

Natty Man

There is an older man who strolls through my neighborhood most every morning, heading to the corner market to pick up his paper.

I always look for him because he makes me feel good about growing older. He is everything I think a man in his eighties should be. And that's natty.

He wears a straw hat with a wide brim, a bow tie, a blue and white seersucker suit, and white bucks. Sometimes he wears a white linen suit, properly wrinkled.

But instead of looking like a fool or a dandy or some cartoon character, he carries it off as if he has worn these outfits all his life, which he probably has. He wears them well.

Which brings me to the question of the day. Whatever happened to natty? Whatever happened to jaunty? Whatever happened to at least *attempting* to look good in the summer sun?

Southern men have done well at this for generations. Bless them and their cotton.

And there's a group of New England Yankees who hold their own in the natty category, sipping gin and tonics in their blue blazers and white trousers as the breeze blows in off the sea.

Bless *them* and their Top-Siders.

But by all accounts it appears the ranks of such men are thinning rapidly.

Very rapidly.

The ugly American is no longer going abroad to be ugly. He's ugly right here on his own turf. Look around.

Go to a mall.

Go to the beach.

Go to a ball game.

Don't these men own mirrors?

My mom always said people look better in winter, and she's right. A long heavy coat can hide a multitude of sartorial sins. But summer offers no such camouflage.

All this became painfully clear to me when I went to Disney World last month and quickly realized Mickey Mouse was one of the better-dressed guys in the crowd. For all its powers, the Disney magic does not work on the wardrobes of its guests.

While waiting for a friend, I sat on a bench outside the Magic Kingdom and decided, just for fun, to see how long it would be before someone natty passed my way—someone who had actually thought about what he put on that morning. Someone with just a hint of style. Someone who knows that a blue blazer takes you everywhere and that the white bucks go back in the closet on Labor Day.

I wasn't asking for my elderly neighbor. I knew I wouldn't see a seersucker suit, but some linen pants and a crisp white shirt would have been nice. I would have settled for pressed khaki shorts and a white T-shirt from the Gap.

Heck, by the end of my game, I would have settled for matching socks.

But it was a fool's errand.

Natty never appeared.

Khaki never came by.

After I counted thirty-nine men in tank tops and those football coach shorts with the Sansabelt waist, I packed it in and called it a day.

Maybe natty doesn't count anymore. I don't know. Maybe I'm stuck in a frame from a Merchant-Ivory film and can't get out. Maybe I'm hoping my own white bucks, if I click the heels together three times, will take me back to a time when people actually dressed as if they were going to be seen in public, even if they weren't.

Not that there aren't young men who don't *try* these days. There are. The look they're going for is something entirely different, however. It's not natty. It's nerdy. But you have to give them credit for at least trying.

I go to a trendy place to get my hair cut—so trendy I don't need to read magazines to find out what's hip. I just have to go there and it all becomes perfectly clear.

Everyone who works at the salon is into the fashion of the minute, not just the day. All have fallen victim to it.

The young man who checks me in has very short hair, a ring in his nose, and industrial-strength black shoes.

The other day he was wearing the "look" that's so popular these days with those young enough not to remember it from the first time it appeared.

Call it geek chic.

Tight nylon shirt. Polyester pants. Retro '70s, I guess.

I didn't like the look the first time out, and it hasn't improved with age. Why someone wants to look like the Math Club president in a 1971 yearbook photo I don't have a clue, but he does. The only thing that's missing is the slide rule, not that any of them would have a clue as to what a slide rule is or was.

As the stylist was clipping away, I could only think of my neighbor in his seersucker suit, and I asked myself these questions.

Fifty years from now, will an old man walk to the neighborhood store for his morning paper wearing polyester pants, a tight nylon shirt, and clunky black shoes?

And fifty years from now, will a younger neighbor look at him and smile, thinking how wonderful it is to be that cool at that age?

I don't think so. But I've been wrong before. I once owned a leisure suit.

Glancing in Windows at Night

I was walking the streets of Boston's Beacon Hill a while ago, looking in windows.

Glancing up at a beautiful chandelier through the fan window over the door of a handsome Federal town house, I noticed the color of the hallway. It was a bright yellow—the exact bright yellow I had been looking for. I had seen it in a magazine but could never replicate it in a paint store.

What to do? I wondered. I can't ring the doorbell and say, "By the way, I've been looking in your window, and I wonder what color that is in your hallway."

Just then the door opened and a lovely woman with an even lovelier young daughter stepped out, looking for all the world as if they were on their way to Miss Porter's School.

She looked at me and asked if she could help. (The question was part polite, part "isn't-it-time-you-moved-along, buddy?")

"Well, to be honest, you can," I said. "What brand of paint is that bright yellow color in your hallway?"

The woman burst out laughing.

"I can't tell you how many people ask me questions about the house, people just like you looking in from the street."

Little did she know there are millions of us—millions of us who glance into windows from the street.

Come on, admit it. You do it, too. I see you glancing in my kitchen window all the time. We all do it. It's okay. Really, it is.

At a dinner party the other night, everyone around the table confessed they had "glanced" at one time or other.

We are not to be confused with Peeping Toms, who give us glancers a bad name. I, for one, have no interest in seeing strangers in their pajamas. It's unsettling enough seeing old friends in theirs when they come to visit.

But I do have to say I love the early nightfall of winter, when the lights come on at five, illuminating kitchens, living rooms, entryways. Walking the dog, riding in a car, running to the store for a quart of milk, each window I pass unveils a one-act play, a vignette, a tableau of daily life.

Who are these people? I ask. Did they have a good day? What are they cooking for dinner? Why did they paint their living room bright pink, or did they inherit that color? Where did they get that great chair?

I have a suburban friend who takes her dog on long walks at night, brandy snifter in hand, looking for decorating ideas as she strolls her sprawling development.

I live in a neighborhood where all the houses are right on the sidewalk, so I have an advantage. It's not as if I have to go out of my way, walk across lawns to get a closer look, which, by the way, is against all the rules of window-glancing. One never goes out of one's way to glance.

The window is just there.

And one never lingers. You keep moving. Like I said, we're not *weird.* Okay?

But I might slow down a bit if I see a great piece of art over a fireplace, a group of people laughing around a dining room table, a great striped wallpaper.

Sometimes, though, something is so amazing that it brings me to a complete halt. A lime-green entryway a few blocks from my house comes to mind.

Often, there's a scene being played out, a frame from a silent movie. A husband and wife talking over their day, sharing a glass of wine at the kitchen counter. Kids chasing each other up the stairs. A ten-year-old banging away at the piano with a vengeance.

It's like watching a play unfold. There is an air of mystery to it all, no playbill to help you figure out the cast of characters.

That's why I find my winter evening dog walks more intriguing than my Sunday afternoon outings.

On Sundays, I often attend real estate open houses—listen, you get your entertainment where you can—but in truth there's really no fun in it because you're actually *in* the house.

Nothing kills fantasy quicker than the reality of someone's laundry room.

It's the difference between having a crush on someone and having an affair with them. On Sundays, you get to know too much. All intrigue is wiped away.

But at night, strolling by a dark-red living room with an orchid blooming in the window, everything seems so alluring. Maybe there's a fire in the fireplace. Maybe there's witty conversation. Maybe there's ice clinking in crystal glasses.

Maybe I should just get a life of my own, you say?

Maybe I should.

But not just yet.

Maybe come daylight saving time.

Halloween in the Country

Growing up in the country has its advantages. Trick-or-treating is not one of them.

I remember how envious I was of the kids in town, the ones who had hundreds of houses to go to. I had images of them running from porch to lighted porch, bags so filled with candy they had to be dragged along.

I grew up on a farm, but our place was on the edge of a hamlet of ten houses, population fifty-two. The place was so small we couldn't even be called a crossroads because the two roads we had didn't cross. They only made a T.

On Halloween, the pickings were slim. Auntie Bernice, over on the other road, gave out popcorn balls, which to an eight-year-old in the country seemed quite exotic. They were in plastic wrap, tied up with orange ribbon. The rest of the lot weren't so creative, offering nothing more original than M&M's. One neighbor gave out dimes. One dime per kid. Yes, she was odd.

But whatever we got was never enough to even cover the bottom of the bag. We could have held all the Halloween candy we gathered in a small lunch bag, but having the optimism of youth, year after year, we lugged shopping bags. It didn't help matters any that two houses never gave out anything, their porch lights as dark as the owners' spirit.

The whole trick-or-treat journey could be done in less than twenty minutes. Then we'd return home, all dressed up with no place left to go.

In the meantime, the older kids, which included my brother and his gang of rabble-rousers, were out being creative—soaping windows and toilet-papering trees. They were twelve. Far too cool to trick-or-treat.

One year, their Halloween shenanigans got the better of them when they overturned Laverne Hall's outhouse and in their panic to escape found themselves falling into the hole. My biggest regret in life is I wasn't there to witness it. To make matters better, they had to be hosed down before they could enter the house.

My pal Patty Miller often accompanied me on my Halloween rounds. She lived up the road and viewed our trick-or-treat situation as I did. Pathetic.

So one year, we decided we would branch out. We would not be confined by the borders of our dreary little life. We would walk down roads not taken.

I was an Appaloosa horse that year. Brown and white. My costume's mask was so long that whenever I moved my head quickly, I bumped into things, like Patty Miller. The tail was so long, it needed to be held.

Patty was a hobo, so when I wasn't bumping her with my horse head, she was hitting me with the hobo stick that rested on her shoulder. We were a vaudeville act, trapped in the farmlands of upstate New York.

Once we finished the ten houses, we made our move. There were a couple of houses half a mile down the road. Untapped territory. We would go to them, get more candy, and keep moving. Maybe we'd walk all the way into town, eight miles away.

The fact that we both were terrified was never discussed. It didn't need to be. I remember cars barreling down the highway toward us. We must have been a sight. A hobo clutching an Appaloosa clutching his own tail. But no one stopped. No one even slowed down.

When we approached one of the houses we'd never been to before, we saw the porch light was on. Our hearts raced. Then, all of a sudden, out of the sky, maybe a tree, fell two bodies. They could have been ghosts.

What followed was panic, chaos, and mayhem.

I wet my Appaloosa horse costume right there on the spot. And Patty Miller? She screamed a scream so long and so loud that I could believe it was still going on, except for the fact I saw her last year and she appears to have finally pulled herself together.

My brother, however, is *still* laughing.

Winter

Cousin Georgie

My family is very small. My mom. A brother. An aunt and two cousins. So when one of my cousins died this month, I headed home.

Georgie, as I still called him, although he would have turned sixty soon, suffered minimal brain damage at birth. He stuttered, never graduated from high school, and worked at a grocery store named Jubilee. He loved it there, driving through the early-morning darkness to open the place, to make sure the shopping carts were all in order, to greet the first customers of the day who stopped by for the morning paper and a doughnut.

Although we grew up less than a mile apart, we were never close. As a kid, I was probably embarrassed by him, impatient with his slow speech. And then I went off to college and another life, seeing him only once a year or so whenever I came home and stopped by the store to pick up some milk.

I'm sorry about that now, sorry I didn't make more of an effort to get to know him better. But he was an independent sort, stubborn some would say, and very content being alone.

He had his cats, his cigars, his Buffalo Bills, and the sub sandwich he'd pick up on his way home from work. It was dinner more often than not. Just a few days before he died, he asked if a co-worker could bring him one to the hospital.

My mom and brother and I visited him there Christmas Day, but almost immediately he told us we'd better get home. As usual, he was worried about the weather. A storm was always looming in Georgie's world.

They say the family is often the last to really know its members. Maybe they're right. As people came through the funeral home, they told stories of a man I never knew.

There was the story about a woman who broke her hip while doing the "Jubilee Shuffle" with him.

There were people who said he knew which shopping cart they wanted, although for the life of me I don't know how he could tell one from another.

And there was the woman at the post office who said he'd often bring her cookies, although she'd always protest.

"Oh, George, I'm on a diet," she'd say.

"You need your energy," he'd reply.

He was the first person many saw in the morning, and to them that was a great comfort.

They said it will be very odd not to see him standing there by Jubilee's front door.

Georgie was also known for handing out root-beer barrels, those hard sugar candies from another era. Seventy pounds of them were found in his apartment. Maybe he was cornering the market. We don't know, but during calling hours, there was a basket of them at the end of the casket. People put them in their pockets, one last treat from a friend.

After the service, where he was laid out in the red and blue of the Buffalo Bills, my brother and I, along with men from the supermarket, carried him to his grave.

And then we gathered at the local Methodist church for a

luncheon of ham and scalloped potatoes, green bean casse-role, and three types of Jell-O. Orange. Lime. Cherry. Each with the appropriate fruit floating inside.

A simple end to a far-from-simple life.

Waiting for a Snowstorm

Having grown up in snow country, a good old-fashioned winter storm is something I embrace rather than flee. To me there is something comforting about a big storm heading my way. I get giddy just thinking about it. Throw another log on the fire, pull a good book off the shelf, put a pot of stew on the stove, and I'm ready to settle in for the duration.

The big storm that roared through the middle of the country earlier this month was promised here on the East Coast, too, but it never arrived in Washington. It went to Buffalo instead. It's still there.

I stood in my living room window most of New Year's weekend, waiting for the heavens to unload. It turned out to be my own sad staging of *Waiting for Godot*. It sputtered. It spit. But it never amounted to a thing. A flop of a snowstorm if I ever saw one. Or, in this case, didn't see.

Not that some of the local municipalities didn't get out their plows to show taxpayers they're getting their money's worth. A rural Virginia county west of here got a dusting of snow and there, on the six o'clock news, was a snowplow scraping a bare road, sparks flying.

What's going on here? I wondered. Plow envy? What do

they want to do, play with the big boys from Buffalo—snow or no snow? I could only laugh.

I know that people who didn't grow up with snow get nervous at even the mention of the word, but I mean, really, folks, pull yourselves together. It's only snow.

I quickly realized I was living in Oz when I moved here fourteen years ago and the morning radio disc jockeys announced school closings *before* there was even a sighting of the first snowflake. I didn't know this at the time, so imagine my surprise when I opened the blinds that morning expecting a storm swirling outside my window and saw nothing. Not a thing. It was clear as could be.

Nothing has changed.

As usual, the talk of a storm worked people here into a frenzy over the weekend. As you all know, we in Washington can work ourselves into a frenzy over most anything. Sex. Impeachment. An impending snowstorm.

For days the TV anchors were telling us about the storm heading our way. They were oh so earnest about its severity. They also were oh so wrong. But that didn't stop the stations from airing "team" coverage of that one snowflake that fell.

"The roads are *wet!*" a reporter relayed back to the station with great urgency.

On the night before the storm was to arrive, there were the usual reports on TV from area supermarkets about the rush to buy milk, bread, bottled water, and toilet paper. The film on the eleven o'clock news showed nothing but empty shelves at the local Safeway. The locust had descended.

"Just stocking up for the storm," a frantic shopper told the reporter.

Now, I understand the milk. I understand the bread. I

understand the bottled water. But for the life of me, I have never understood this stockpiling of toilet paper during a snowstorm.

How long do these people think they will be snowed in? How much toilet paper do they need? What do these people eat during a snowstorm that would warrant fighting over that last jumbo twelve-roll pack of Charmin?

Does a good old-fashioned snowstorm bring on an unpleasant ailment I'm not aware of—an ailment where toilet paper is indeed something you don't want to be without? If so, I've never experienced it in my forty-nine years on this earth, many of them spent in the Snow Belt of western New York. Believe me, if there were such a malady, I'd know about it.

I remember as a kid being snowed in for a week. It was a huge storm—snow followed by ice followed by more snow. The roads were closed. School was closed. We had no heat and slept on the living room floor in front of the fireplace. Our elderly neighbors, Walter and Lena, joined us because they not only had no heat, but no fireplace, either. Six of us played cards and ate soup and made popcorn over the fire. And, by God, we were all as regular as a clock.

But not once do I remember my father saying, "God, this is getting really bad. We're running low on toilet paper!"

We were a stronger people back then.

The String Drawer

It doesn't happen very often, but every now and then I have the urge to clean out a drawer. It happened just the other night.

I was cleaning up after dinner, putting stuff in the dishwasher, when I opened up a kitchen drawer. The string drawer.

It's not called the string drawer because it holds only string. It's called the string drawer because it takes miles and miles of string to hold everything in there together. Pull up the string at any point and everything comes with it. Flashlights. Screwdrivers. A petrified pretzel from another century. It's all quite handy.

I grew up in a house that had such a drawer—a drawer that held an amazing collection of disparate items brought together by nothing more than fate and held together by nothing more than string. We'd go there and, more often than not, find what we needed.

Thumbtacks. Dental floss. Age-old bubble gum.

I'll be honest. The only reason I cleaned out the string drawer the other night was because I couldn't close it. Everything in it seemed to come to life once the drawer was opened, none of it willing to quietly retreat to where it came from. So the excavation began.

I'm always a bit surprised when I find things in my own home I've never seen before—but there it was, a dish towel with the U.S. Capitol painted on it. Don't have a clue where it came from. And there was a seed packet for an herb I've never heard of or tasted. Opened, too.

But everything else looked vaguely familiar. There were two little American flags left over from a Fourth of July picnic, a Dunkin' Donuts key chain, a paint-chip strip with colors ranging from "lemonade" to "Nantucket yellow." We went with neither.

I was happy to uncover a small flashlight given out at the Lillehammer Olympics, not only because I have fond memories of Norway, but because it still works. And there were matches from restaurants across the nation, matches I anally arranged in a little bowl while reminiscing about lovely expense-account dinners at each.

There was half a window latch, a solitary glass cocktail stirrer, two lapel pins in the shape of vodka bottles, and a napkin from Bobby Van's Steakhouse, a place I've never been. Digging deeper, I came upon seven chopsticks, a ribbon from a Dean & DeLuca pastry box, and a couple of photos, one of people I do not know, although they appear to be sitting at my dining room table. With me.

The other photo was of my friend Eileen and her three children, taken so long ago they were still listening to her.

And stuck to the bottom of the drawer with melted peppermint candy was a postcard from my friend Pam. The photo was of the library in York Harbor, Maine. Her message was to have a good time on vacation. The postmark was 1986.

You wouldn't recognize the drawer today. *I* don't recognize the drawer today. Dish towels are folded and stacked in the corner, the matches are in their little bowl, the chopsticks all have a mate, and the unruly string has been tamed into a tidy ball.

Problem is, I can't find a thing anymore.

Department Stores

The magic of the day has no doubt grown stronger over the years, but a friend of mine says the best day of her life was a late November Saturday about forty years ago when her mother took her into the city and bought her a bright blue winter coat at Lord & Taylor.

The two went to the department store's tearoom for lunch, strolled up Fifth Avenue to gaze at the store's Christmas windows, and then caught the train home.

The fact she still calls it "the best day of my life" more than irritates her husband, who asks where their wedding day ranks.

"Not even close," she replies. This would be funny except that it's true.

I was at their wedding. It was a lovely affair and she truly seemed very happy. But I understand. A wedding, no matter how long the open bar remains open, can't hold a candle to the magic of a department store during the holidays.

I am a department store junkie. If I'm in a city with a famous store, I'll go there almost immediately. Wanamaker's in Philadelphia. Macy's in New York. Dayton's in Minneapolis.

Each has its own personality, its own quirkiness, its own

sense of style. They are the great shrines to shopping, built before it was a contact sport, when clerks were not only present, but actually happy to help.

I grew up in the aisles of Sibley, Lindsey & Curr Company in Rochester, New York. I don't have a clue who Sibley, Lindsey, and Curr were, but that doesn't matter. They ran a fine operation.

It was grand in an old-world way, with terrazzo floors and polished wood benches near the revolving doors. There were even men running the elevators, pulling back the iron gate and announcing each floor as if all their passengers were blind.

There was also a huge copper four-sided clock that hung from the ceiling near the main-floor escalators. Every Saturday it was where kids met their mothers following an afternoon of going separate ways.

A clerk who worked the glove counter near the clock would chat us up as we waited for our tardy moms, delayed no doubt by a pair of sexy 7AAs in the shoe department.

Sibley's had everything. Sporting goods near the side door, finer dresses on two, toys on five. Above that was the Tower Restaurant, typical of all department-store tearooms where you could get a breaded veal cutlet with mashed potatoes and Harvard beets for $1.99. There was even a bakery on the main floor, home to such exotic goods as cakes in the shape of cowboys.

I could have lived at Sibley's. Almost did once. One winter's day Mom said we had to leave quickly or we'd be snowed in there. So what's the problem? I asked.

At Christmastime the escalators swept us up to Toyland, where the same man, year after year, played "Jingle Bells" on a kazoo shaped like a tiny toy trombone. It was industrial-strength cacophony, but the first year he wasn't there, something seemed terribly wrong.

It wasn't Christmas until we went to Sibley's, just as it's not Christmas to Chicagoans until they go to Marshall Field's.

When I was ten, my folks took me to Washington, D.C., at Christmastime to see the sights. The only thing I remember from the trip is Garfinkel's department store, with its elegant wood counters topped with what seemed like a legion of lamps, each sporting a white pleated shade. And behind each counter was a sturdy woman dressed in black. Ready and willing to help.

The store's massive columns were wrapped in gold garland that year. Versailles never looked so good.

Twenty-five years later, when I returned to Washington to live, one of the first places I went was Garfinkel's. It was one of the most comforting pilgrimages I've ever made. The lamps and the women in black were still there, none the worse for wear.

Garfinkel's is gone now. So is Sibley's and I. Magnin, Best & Co., Woodie's, and Gimbel's. The list goes on. Grand old department stores are becoming as rare as independent bookstores. An equally sad trend.

Without wishing to sound like an old geezer who spends his days muttering "I remember when," I truly feel sorry for this generation.

What holiday shopping memories are they going to have without a department store to call their own? A romp through the Gap followed by lunch at McDonald's?

Oh, where is the trombone man when we need him most?

The Drive Home for the Holidays

Not many of us go over the river and through the woods to grandmother's house anymore.

If only we could sit back and let the horse who knows the way take us home again. But that's not to be.

Instead, we get in a car and travel long distances to gather with other family members who probably would be more than happy to be back in their own homes.

But that's another story.

For decades now, I have traveled to my childhood home for Christmas, to the house I grew up in, to the house that has the same phone number I used to dial when I missed the bus in third grade.

I have never had Christmas in my own home. At fifty-one, I'm still too young to do that, or at least that's what my mother says. So I go home, which, to be honest, is actually rather nice. My stocking is still on the fireplace, I sleep in my old bedroom, and I still go down to the cellar to get the firewood for the evening fires, firewood my late father stacked against the stone wall.

The only difference now is I drink wine on Christmas Eve instead of milk, which makes everything much jollier. But that's another story, too.

My parents had the excellent sense to settle down in the Snow Belt of western New York, as did their parents and grandparents and great-grandparents. A hardy lot. But then again, they never had to travel very far for Christmas dinner. Just up or down the road, depending on who was hosting. So what did they know?

I never really thought much about the journey until I began driving home every Christmas. One year, the five-hour trip from Saratoga Springs turned into ten. I had a sports car, and my road-hugging grille acted like a snowplow as I slowly made my way west.

Another year, I remember getting halfway home and pulling over in Syracuse when I saw a mile-high wall of snow coming toward me at 50 mph. But I plowed on the next day, determined not to break my home-every-Christmas record.

I grew up driving in snow. I pretty much know the tricks of the trade, so I'm always a bit surprised when I have a passenger who doesn't quite understand what's going on.

A couple of years ago, on the eight-hour ride from Washington, we were but a mile or so from my parents' home when we found ourselves in a whiteout. So close, I thought. Yet so far.

For those with little or no knowledge of winter storms, a whiteout is when you can see nothing but white. Nothing. The car is encircled in a sea of white.

Aside from the fact it's incredibly dangerous to be driving a car on a road where you can see nothing, it's actually sort of cool.

I slowed to a crawl. You're supposed to keep moving, since you never know when a tractor-trailer is behind you, ready to ride up your trunk if you decide to stop.

I was inching along at 5 mph when my passenger—my partner, Jack—lost it.

"Stop! Stop!" he yelled out. "I can't see a thing!"

I did what any driver would do under the circumstances. I slapped him with the back of my right hand, never taking my eyes off the world of white outside.

And over the river and through the woods we crawled. Home for the holidays.

The Perfect Tree

I took it for granted as a kid, going out across the fields and through the orchards to chop down a Christmas tree. We did it every year. I never thought a thing about it.

It all seems a little too Ralph Lauren now. Dad in his red-and-black-checked jacket, ax over his shoulder. Me trudging behind, trying to catch up. But that's the way it was. I didn't realize then that my childhood Christmas tree hunt would be fodder for magazine ads by the end of the century.

Our destination was a conservation pond surrounded by fir trees on the far side of the Red Delicious orchard. It was there, year after year, that we went in search of the perfect Christmas tree.

The afternoon would always start out pleasantly enough—Dad wanting to cut down the first tree he saw, me asking for a little more time to check out a few more trees down the way.

Anyone who has ever hunted for the perfect Christmas tree knows it takes time. One can't be rushed. But by the time we had circled the pond three times, my father's Christmas spirit was pretty much spent.

"There are no perfect trees, Craig, just as there are no perfect sons," he once said through clenched teeth. Even as a child, I understood his message immediately and chose the next tree I saw, realizing at that point I could easily be an orphan by Christmas morning. The annual challenge never changed—to find the perfect tree before my father ran out of patience or the sun went down, whichever came first.

Some years the two coincided.

We came home with a variety of trees over the years, and, I have to say, none came close to meeting my high standards.

But when Dad was dragging one toward the house, I always thought the same thing: "This is it, this is the perfect tree, this is the one I'll remember for the rest of my life."

When the tree got into the house, however, reality quickly set in.

One was so ugly it still leaps out at me from the black-and-white holiday photos from that Christmas long ago. I have no idea what happened. Maybe it was covered with snow at the time and I didn't see the huge hole in its right side—a hole so huge four boxes of tinsel from Murphy's Five & Dime couldn't disguise it.

Another was so tall Dad had to chop off the top third of it to allow it to stand up straight in the living room, leaving the impression that the rest of the tree had broken through the ceiling and could be viewed upstairs in my brother's bedroom.

And yet another had osteoporosis so bad it had to be tied to the windowsill with binding twine to keep it from falling across the living room floor. It stood so straight and proud out at the pond. I have no idea what happened once it got inside.

But as they say, each had its own charms, and for some mysterious reason, each succeeded in carrying out the role of the Wilson family tree with grace and aplomb. They had personality. I guess Christmas trees are like brides: There are no ugly ones.

Today my Christmas tree hunting isn't quite so romantic. We go to a vacant lot next to the local Boys Club, where trees miraculously sprout a couple of weeks before Christmas.

The operation is run by a bunch of affable men who follow me around and hold the trees up for inspection. They are patient and kind. They have seen my type before.

"What about that one?" I will ask, and they will lean over and pull a Douglas fir or Fraser fir or Scotch pine up to its feet.

And then I will say no and move on down the line.

I can still go on for hours in my quest for the perfect tree, but I try to control myself, abiding by my childhood rules. I will stay only until sundown or until someone clenches his teeth.

Actually, the whole process isn't anywhere near as hard as it was when I was a kid.

The trees today are far more perfect than any we cut down back home on the farm, all grown and trimmed and pruned now for the sole purpose of bearing baubles and beads.

Each is a beauty.

But for some reason, none seems as pretty.

Aluminum Christmas Trees

When I was growing up, few people I knew had good taste. Not that I was sure what good taste was, but I knew it when I saw it, and I didn't see it very often. Especially at Christmastime.

Good taste was something special, something not seen every day, something a little different. At least that was my definition at ten.

Living on a farm, I longed for the city life, where I was sure good taste lurked on every street corner. I discovered years later that wasn't true.

All I knew was that our annual misshapen Christmas tree, cut down out on the back forty, was nothing but common.

Everyone had a similar one, everyone decorated it exactly the same, everyone accepted the fact that it came with either a lighted star or a tired-looking angel in a tattered white gown on top.

I knew there had to be more.

So imagine my delight when, riding into town with my folks one night to look at the holiday lights, I saw what could only be described as a vision—an aluminum Christmas tree. It was in the picture window of a local family's house, a family my father used to call avant-garde.

I didn't have a clue what avant-garde was, but I assumed it

was French for good taste. I found out later it meant they were Democrats.

As if that shimmering tree weren't beautiful enough, the family gilded the silver lily, decorating it with nothing but pink satin balls. It was lighted from below or behind or from somewhere above, and it looked as if it were floating in that window. As I said, it was a vision.

I had never seen such a beautiful thing in all my ten years.

When I got back home that night, the fresh-cut tree we had just hauled into the house and decorated with colored lights and tinsel and the most oddball assortment of ornaments and trinkets—including the red-and-green garland of construction-paper rings I had brought home from school—looked so garish and haphazard that I was embarrassed not only for myself, but for my whole family. I was sure I had been adopted. At least switched at birth. It was then I knew I would become a Democrat.

For the first time, I understood that old line about how hard it is to keep people down on the farm once they've seen those bright city lights. I had traveled to Paris that night, seen what it had to offer—shimmering trees bearing pink satin orbs!—and wanted no more of life on the farm.

Eight years later I left, never to return, secure in the knowledge that nothing but beautiful things were out there waiting for me.

I'm old enough now to understand that "good taste," like beauty, is in the eye of the beholder.

I walked into Restoration Hardware the other day, and there, in the middle of the showroom, was a live Christmas tree strung with those garish red/blue/green/yellow/white/orange lights I grew up with. It also was covered with an oddball assortment of ornaments and trinkets.

It looked a little hokey, very '50s, and a lot like my Christmas trees on the farm.

It was the most beautiful thing I've seen in, let's see, about forty years.

Tinsel

The cover of the December issue of *House & Garden* shows a perfect family trimming the perfect Christmas tree.

Perfect ornaments are hanging from every perfect bough. And as far as I can tell, the perfect family is not only happy and content, but also still speaking.

Obviously, this photo has been doctored. Either that, or the perfect family has been into the spiked eggnog a little early in the season.

Many families I know—and certainly my own memories prove this true—cannot decorate a Christmas tree and still be talking by the time the treetop angel is finally put in her place.

Our family drama would begin shortly after my father and I would drag the tree in. We often would cut our tree down on the farm, selected from a grove of evergreens surrounding the pond. The pickings were sometimes slim. Actually, they were always slim.

This was long before the days of the perfectly shaped Christmas tree in every window, so an occasional branch sticking out here and there didn't strike us as anything odd. It just was.

And that huge hole in the tree's side? Well, that was just a decorating challenge to be filled with as many ornaments and miles of garland as needed.

I was blinded by the bright lights of Christmas. When I look at photos of Christmases past, I can see that some of our trees were indeed downright ugly. Charlie Brown had nothing on the Wilsons of Rural Route 1.

None of this was ever lost on my mother, who would comment on the tree's attributes, or lack thereof, as soon as it was upright in our living room.

"This might just be the ugliest tree you boys ever dragged in," she said one year when our selection happened to have three tops.

We hadn't even noticed.

Such remarks would send my father into his this-is-a-perfectly-fine-tree retort. "All we have to do is get some lights and ornaments on it, and it'll be beautiful," he'd say.

He was right, of course. As I've often said, I'm a firm believer that, like brides, there really is no such thing as an ugly Christmas tree. Some just have more personality than others.

It was all downhill from there. My brother and I would tussle over who got to hang the best ornaments, and when it came time to put on the tinsel, it became all-out war.

He was a one-strand-at-a-time tinsel hanger. Took him forever. I threw the silver strands with abandon, and clumps would soon appear on every bough, a sight that sent my brother around the bend. He followed behind, rehanging each strand.

In retrospect, I might have been doing it on purpose. I don't know. When I finally go into therapy, I'll ask.

Reports are that Christmas tree sales will be very brisk this year. According to the National Christmas Tree Association,

Americans like to gather around the old *Tannenbaum* during times of crisis. There are even reports that we're so into Christmas trees this year, many homes will have two or three, or more.

As if this country hasn't had enough trouble this year.

Opening My Presents Early

Art was one of the hired men on our farm. He worked around the barns mostly, a jack-of-all-trades, mending apple boxes and ladders in the summer and early fall.

We all liked Art.

But I liked Art most in the slower winter months, when he came to the house and baby-sat on Saturday nights. Art was a pushover.

He'd turn on the television, something he didn't have in his own quarters, and settle into an evening of Lawrence Welk and Perry Mason. As long as we remained quiet, we could do anything we wanted. And we did.

It was a few weeks before Christmas, and the excitement was building. Shopping bags seemed to be arriving at the house daily, bags that quickly disappeared behind my parents' bedroom door.

They were nice people, my parents, but not all that clever. There was only one place to hide anything in their bedroom, and that was in a closet tucked under the staircase.

For the most part, I was a good kid, especially at Christmas. I'm not a fool. But one year the pull was too strong. I gave in to temptation one December night when Art was in the living room, soaking in Welk's champagne music.

Before I knew it, I was rummaging around my parents' closet. I was nervous, but I couldn't stop.

Buried under a pile of clothes were bags of Christmas gifts. Pay dirt.

One was a box, the oddest box I'd ever seen; square, but with an extension jutting out one end. I pried it open, and there, inside, sat the most beautiful accordion I'd ever seen. It was red and white plastic, with shiny black and white keys and a bright-turquoise bellow. All the polka bands in Buffalo had nothing like this.

I opened it up and began to play. I did this without fear because among Art's many fine qualities was the fact he couldn't hear very well. You had to shout to get his attention, which of course is a perfect quality for a baby-sitter to have, especially if you're the child.

So, sitting there on the closet floor, I played my little heart out until my arms gave out.

It was then things began to fall apart. I couldn't fold the thing back together. I couldn't get it back in its box. I couldn't control it. It was as if it had come alive, refusing to return to its cage. It was like a jack-in-the-box that wouldn't go down.

It was a nightmare.

I broke out in a cold sweat. My fingerprints were all over this gift. How could I explain to my parents that this thing just popped right out of its traveling case while sitting alone in the closet?

My childhood flashed before my eyes.

Life, as I once knew it, was over.

I can't quite remember how it happened, or how long I remained under the stairs—it seemed an eternity—but I finally jammed the thing back into its case and fled this Pandora's box for good. I was exhausted.

I told Art I was going to bed, which I'm sure he thought was odd, but the other good thing about Art was he asked no questions.

When I came down the stairs on Christmas morning, the accordion, all bright and shiny, sat there under the tree. I could hardly look at it for all the trouble it had caused me. Perplexed, my parents asked me why I wasn't playing with it.

"Later," I said. But later never came. I never played it again. It was cursed.

I had learned my lesson. To this day, I don't sneak around in closets for Christmas gifts.

In retrospect, I came out relatively unscathed. My neighbor Natalie didn't fare so well.

Natalie was younger and not as worldly in these matters as I was. One day, while her mother was away, she opened all the presents under the tree. Every last one of them. There must have been thirty. She was a very busy little girl because then she covered her tracks by rewrapping every last one of them.

In their original state, they sported beautiful bows and crisp corners. When Natalie was done, they looked like they had been run over by a very large train.

This new look did not escape her mother's eye when she returned. She then came over to our house to tell us what Natalie had done and ask what she should do.

"Well, it's already spoiled her Christmas," my mom said. "You don't really need to punish her any more."

For a woman who couldn't hide a Christmas present to save her life, my mom could speak words of brilliance on occasion.

Dad as Santa

I remember at the time thinking he seemed so familiar.

He didn't say much, he never did, but there was something about his lap that made me feel I'd been there before. But as a four-year-old, I thought that was the way Santa's lap should feel. Familiar, comforting, the best lap on earth.

It wasn't until much later that I came to realize Santa and Dad were one and the same, although I think I knew it long before I let on. I was one of those who clung as long as possible to the possibility of Santa Claus.

I still believe.

Dad played Santa for more than forty years. He never took money for it. He never worked for a department store. He never rang a bell outside a grocery store. Instead, he'd dress up for friends and family or anyone else who would call and ask if he'd come by to visit their children on Christmas Eve.

Once I learned to drive I was his chauffeur, waiting in the car as he made his rounds to houses in town or those out on farms on snow-covered plains of western New York. His farmhouse performances were his most impressive.

Dad would get out a quarter mile away from a friend's farm and walk down the road, a bright red figure in a sea of snow white. Santa could never be seen getting out of a Chevy.

When he finally got to the farmhouse, the game plan never changed.

He'd look at the mailbox, or for a house number, as if checking the address to ensure proper delivery later that evening. Then he'd look up and study the pitch of the roof to make sure he and his reindeer could land safely.

By then the kids in the house had spotted him, often with the help of their parents, who would yell that Santa was right outside on the lawn. Some of the kids would rush outside into the snow without a care or a coat. Often they asked Santa where his reindeer were.

"Resting for tonight," he'd always respond.

And then he'd leave, his big black boots making tracks in the snow. He'd walk off down the road, scooting behind a barn or a silo or a thicket of trees where I'd swing by and pick him up.

It was fun driving Santa around. It was like having a celebrity with you. People would wave when they saw him. Or honk their horns. It didn't matter how old they were. No one dared ignore Santa, especially on Christmas Eve.

Years later, when I was out of college and at my first newspaper job five hours away from home, Dad passed through town one December and called to see if I wanted to have dinner. I told him that I couldn't, that I was having a Christmas party but that I'd love him to drop by.

He said he would, and then he impishly added, "I have my suit in the car."

"Wear it," I said.

And he did. No one at the party knew Santa was my dad, and I pretended I didn't have a clue who he was. Just some Santa who wandered in off the street.

One co-worker, who was engaged to another co-worker,

didn't cotton to this Santa who showed up out of nowhere. He thought he was paying too much attention to his fiancée, and when Dad tried to lure her into the hallway to tell her that he was my father, the engaged man quickly followed and pulled her away.

"Not on your life, buster," he said to Santa.

It became one of Dad's favorite Santa stories.

When his own grandchildren arrived, Dad did the duties at his own house on Christmas Eve. He'd disappear to the neighbors to change into his suit and beard and then suddenly, miraculously, appear out on the lawn, looking up at his own roof, once again contemplating the landing approach for later that evening.

His three grandchildren flocked to the window, yelling and waving. But first they had to push me out of the way.

Even at forty I thought a Santa sighting was a good thing on Christmas Eve. I have been known to trample both young and old to get to the window first.

One year, in the excitement of watching Santa wander the lawn, before I knew it I blurted out to my niece and nephews, "Wave to Grandpa!"

One of them turned quickly and corrected me.

"That's not Grandpa! It's Santa!"

And so it was.

Visiting Aunt Elaine

I went to visit my aunt on Christmas Day. She has Alzheimer's and is in a nursing home.

She didn't know me. I could have been anyone.

But I spotted her immediately from way down the hall. Even sitting in a wheelchair she is still a tall woman. She was near the main nurses' station, obviously placed there so she could watch and be watched.

She wore a Christmas sweater, slacks, and an expression as blank as an empty slate. Her trademark no-nonsense black laced shoes with their sturdy block heels were replaced with bedroom slippers. Her white hair was brushed back from her face, a softer style than the one she used to get every week at the beauty shop in town.

She is my only aunt. She lived up the road when I was growing up, a main character in the play that was my childhood. Often I would get off the bus, check in at home, and then walk up to her house. We would talk about my day. We'd have cookies. She'd have tea. I had milk.

In winter we'd do projects, like making construction-paper characters with patterns from the keep-the-kids-busy page in the back of *McCall's.* A Santa with cotton-ball beard we made more than forty years ago still hangs on the family Christmas tree.

In summer we'd sit on the porch and feed the cats that wandered up from the barn. And then the phone would ring, my mother calling me home for dinner.

It seems strange to sit next to her now and not have her say anything to me. I look for a glimmer in her eyes that maybe she recognizes me, but there is none. She keeps her own counsel these days.

But I can still hear her voice. It was strong, almost loud. Sometimes it seemed as if she was shouting, but she wasn't. It was just her voice. When her card club gathered, you could hear her above everyone else.

It was a voice that served her well during her tenure as president of the local school board.

Although she never went to college, she was a walking encyclopedia. She knew the family tree better than anyone. She knew the county better than anyone, too. She knew who was related to whom, who farmed what farm back during the war, who went to Albion High in 1932, correcting my uncle and father whenever they had their facts wrong.

She was efficient the way farm women are efficient.

In season she canned dozens of jars of fruits and vegetables. For days her kitchen counter would be filled with row upon row of them.

During harvest, when we worked in the orchards, she'd have lunch ready on the screened porch. Bowls of sliced peaches. Strawberries. Tomato sandwiches on white bread. Iced tea and lemonade. Cookies.

In winter she sewed in the corner of the kitchen. Rips, tears, missing buttons were all taken care of with a whirl of her Singer. She hemmed the pants of my Cub Scout uniform.

Later in life she worked in the county clerk's office as an abstractor, assisting surveyors whenever land was being transferred. She climbed ladders and lugged huge ledgers down from shelves that climbed to the ceiling. She liked knowing what was going on.

She had good contacts at the motor vehicle bureau, too. It was downstairs from her office in the tiny county complex. She's the one who told me, at sixteen, that I had passed my driver's test—the best news a country boy could hear.

And when I went to college, she wrote me long letters.

She survived brain surgery in her twenties.

She survived breast cancer in her sixties.

She even survived my long hair and beard in the early '70s. She liked the beard. Didn't care much for the hair.

And before she broke her hip in her eighties, she sat on the floor with me and ate dinner at a Japanese restaurant as if she'd done it every day of her life.

Now she sits in silence.

She has a bulletin board in her room at the nursing home. On it are photos of her son and daughter, grandchildren, and great-grandchildren. And there's one of me, with her, at my parents' fiftieth wedding anniversary a few years ago. She was fading away even then, but there's a smile on her face in the photo.

The smile is gone now. So is the woman I once knew.

I never thought you could miss someone who is sitting right next to you.

I was wrong.

Life's Luxuries

This month's *Town & Country* has a feature called "What Is Luxury?"

In it, a number of rich and famous people were asked to share their thoughts on what luxury meant to them. Some talked of yachts on the Mediterranean, Egyptian linen sheets on the bed, nights on the beach at Cap Juluca.

Others, like conductor André Previn, said luxury was a house without phones. A man after my own heart.

But interior designer Victoria Hagan perhaps gave the most interesting response: "It's the things that money can't buy." She's right, of course. Luxury has nothing to do with what can be purchased on Madison Avenue, although that pistachio-colored cashmere sweater I saw at Paul Stuart last month felt pretty good. But as my dad used to say, "It's just stuff."

Was "luxury" under your tree this Christmas? Or has it been right outside your back door all along?

A garden would be the ultimate luxury for me, probably since I don't have one. I would love nothing more than to spend the new year puttering around a small plot of land, tending some flowers, some sweet corn, some zucchini. Well, maybe not zucchini. Sunflowers. Big, gaudy, bawdy sunflowers all in a row.

That would be luxury.

I don't have a lilac bush, either. I think a lilac bush is pure luxury. Right along with an elegant boxwood hedge, rhubarb out behind the barn, a row of iris along a fence, a raspberry bush.

I'm much more jealous of someone's raspberry bush than their jewelry. Anyone can have diamonds. Not everyone has a raspberry bush.

Living next to a young child is a luxury. My neighbor Benny, almost two now, greets me most mornings, grabbing on to my stair railing, yelling out my name, beckoning me to come out to play. If only I had the time.

Time, of course, is the ultimate luxury. No use having the garden if you have no time to toil in it. No use having a lilac bush if you can't stop and smell it. No use having a child next door if you can't go swing on command.

Pure luxury is time to read the whole paper in the morning, time to take long walks with the dog, time to have long lunches with friends on rainy afternoons when there's no place to go, no schedule to keep. Better than a rushed breakfast at Tiffany's any day.

Forget Cap Juluca, the yacht, the suite at the Mercer Hotel. Luxury is a cottage at the lake with a dog sleeping on the dock and an Adirondack chair with your name on it. A Ralph Lauren tableau without the Ralph Lauren price tag.

Even the editors of *Town & Country* confessed that true luxury is not expensive. It's priceless.

A clothesline, rain on the roof, a steady wind in your sails, a good old-fashioned snowstorm, especially if you live where you don't get one every week. Add a roaring fire, a jigsaw puzzle, and the inability to go anywhere for a couple of days, and it doesn't get much better than that.

But perhaps the greatest luxury of all is living a good life without ever quite knowing what Egyptian linen sheets might be.

New Year's Resolutions

I don't make New Year's resolutions anymore. I'm old enough to know better.

For the most part they're broken before the hangover is gone, which is particularly troubling to those who annually resolve to cut back on the drinking.

We've heard them all: Lose weight. Take better care of yourself. Make new friends. Find a faithful companion. Get more exercise. Take in a lost soul. Get to know your neighbors.

I have a better one, and it covers all the resolutions above.

Get a dog.

Just go to the pound and get a dog.

Oh, I can hear what you're saying right now. "The last thing I need in my life right now is a dog."

You're wrong.

It's the *first* thing you need.

Too busy? Too busy for what? A little more love in your life? Maybe that's your problem. Maybe you've been looking for love in all the wrong places. A dog will treat you better than anyone you'll meet at happy hour. Trust me. I've been to happy hour.

In a perfect world, every dog would have a home and every

home would have a dog. And believe me, it would be a better world.

If President Clinton had gotten his dog a bit sooner than he did, he might not be in the mess he's in today. Dogs protect their owners from every kind of trouble, including themselves.

Besides, they're a lot cheaper than mistresses.

Yes, dogs are responsibilities, but what's wrong with a little responsibility? FDR had time for Fala, his Scottie, and he was running a country at war.

Yes, you have to walk them, but what's wrong with a walk every morning? Built-in exercise.

Yes, you have to plan for their care when you go away. So? As any dog owner will tell you, it's a small price to pay for total devotion.

Get a dog.

You'll get more kisses than you ever imagined. You'll never be lonely again. You'll always have someone to talk to. Dogs are great listeners. Some of the best conversations I've ever had have been with my dog Murphy.

The whole tenor of your life will change—from the smell of the dog's warm breath on your face as she stands by the bed, silently announcing the beginning of your day, to the sound of four feet galloping down the hallway when you put the key in the door at night. These are good things. Again, trust me.

A dog will quickly turn you into a fool, but who cares? Better your dog than your boss. I'm a fool for my dog and proud of it.

You'll live longer. Your house will be dirtier, but your blood pressure will be lower.

You will laugh more. Both at yourself and at your dog.

You will increase your circle of friends. "Dog people" will enter your life. This, too, is good.

Even here in workaholic Washington, the dog people have their priorities straight. They know work can wait another thirty minutes. There are more important things to do.

Like throwing sticks.

Who would you rather spend time with? A dog or a politician? Case closed.

You see things differently with a dog at your side.

Like life.

Dogs stop and smell the bushes. They give tours of back alleys and neighborhood lanes you never knew existed. They make you linger.

Dogs are better than children. Even my friends with children say that. As a dog friend of mine likes to say, children are for people who can't have dogs.

They rarely talk back, their education costs far less, they come with their own clothes, and they always eat what they're served. Plus, dogs appreciate every last thing you do for them.

So, how about it?

It's a new year.

Get a new life.

Get a dog.

A Tent in Winter

My neighbor Ethan embraces life with the enthusiasm of a five-year-old, which is what he is.

"Hey, Craig!" he'll yell if he catches me leaving my house. "Where you goin'?"

At times, he seems to be everywhere. Out on the sidewalk. At our neighborhood corner store. Taking in the scene from the backseat of his dad's car. And often I'll look out my front window and find him waving at me from his living room window across the street, the greeting made even more enthusiastic by his bouncing up and down on the sofa. His zest for life never ceases to amuse me.

The other day I happened to peer from the upstairs window, and, instead of seeing Ethan's bouncing wave, I noticed something was covering most of his parents' living room floor. It was red and blue and square. After a couple of seconds, I realized it was a freestanding pup tent with nylon mesh windows, curved aluminum rods, and zippers galore.

When I saw his mother a few days later and asked about the tent, she said Ethan had taken up residence there during the recent blizzard. It had become a permanent fixture. Before long, she feared, he would be taking all his meals in the tent, sleeping in the tent, entertaining his friends in the tent. It was where he was cocooning until spring, she said, venturing out only to hunt the bears he said roam their town house.

A boy after my own heart.

I didn't have anything as fancy as a tent—complete with lantern, jackknife, and ax, no less—to entertain me during the long winter snowstorms of western New York. I had to be much more enterprising. I used my parents' furniture.

As soon as the man on the Buffalo radio station announced school was closed for the day, the living room chairs were turned on their heads, sofa cushions became padded walls, and sheets and towels were pulled from the closet. Roofing.

In no time, the living room was transformed into a North African *souk*, a mysterious maze of narrow and dark crawl spaces to be explored, and eventually defended from older brothers and other enemies.

I remember feeling safe and secure in there, sitting under the turned-over wingback chair, surrounded by pillows and blankets and the collection of maps and manuals a five-year-old has to show him the way.

I'm not quite sure where my mother was during all this. But my theory would be that if this kept me occupied during a long, snowy day off from school, it was worth her looking the other way, no matter what her living room ended up looking like by dinnertime.

To her mind, putting up with a room of makeshift forts and tunnels was a lot better than having to remove my boots and snow pants half a dozen times as I came and went from the sledding fields outside.

The woman was not a fool.

Romance Is in the Cards

I was picking out my Valentine cards the other day, minding my own business, when a man came up and just stood next to me. I tried to ignore him, but he would not be ignored. When I finally turned to look at him, he handed me a card.

"This good?" he asked in beginner's English.

I looked at the card, one of those over-the-top, let's-make-a-big-impression-on-my-new-girlfriend cards, and I said it was indeed a good card if it was for his fiancée.

"Yes, fiancée," he said.

But for some reason, I had a hunch this man did not have a fiancée.

"So, when are you getting married?" I asked.

"No, not getting married," he quickly responded. "Girlfriend."

It was then I told him we'd best put the fiancée card back on the mile-long wall of cards and look for something more generic.

"Generic?" he asked.

"Yes," I said. "A card you can give without having to marry the person."

He liked this idea, nodded his head, and started taking

cards out of the rack with wild abandon, putting them in my hand, asking me to analyze each and every one.

One, I told him, was for a man. He laughed and shook his head no. We put it back.

Another was for a mother.

"In Ethiopia," he said.

We put it back, although I told him I thought it would be a nice idea if he dropped her a card every now and then. He sheepishly agreed.

And many of the cards he chose were of the humorous variety, or the allegedly humorous variety.

"Don't you want to be more romantic than that?" I asked, handing back a card that showed "The Looove Doctor—No Appointment Needed!"

"Yes, romantic," he replied.

This exercise went on for a few more minutes until he finally settled on another huge let's-make-a-big-impression five-dollar card bearing a large red flower on the front. For the One I Love, it read.

"Do you love her?" I asked.

"Yes," he said, smiling one of those beautiful smiles only Ethiopians seem to have.

"Well, then, I think this is your card," I said.

But he was not ready to settle on this card just yet. He wanted me to read to him what was written inside, which I did. It was quite lengthy, dealing with matters of the heart— love, devotion, strength, forever. You've read it before. He nodded his head as I read the verse out loud.

"Good?" he asked.

"Well, it's not Auden, but it'll work," I said.

"Auden?" he asked. He looked confused and a tad disappointed, so I quickly changed my tune.

"Yes, good," I said. "Very good."

He thanked me profusely and shook my hand. I wished him well.

It was then he made a gesture, as if putting a wedding ring on his finger.

"Next year," I said.

"Next year," he said. "Fiancée!"

Spring

Peeps

When I was growing up, the only thing I ever wanted in my Easter basket was Peeps. Dozens and dozens of Peeps. Forget the chocolate Easter bunny. Forget the eggs. I didn't even care if it had that green plastic grass. I just wanted Peeps. Still do.

A symphony of marshmallow and sugar, what more could a junk-food junkie ask for, except maybe more Peeps and a free dental plan.

My friend Jayne has a weakness for Peeps, too, but she likes them only after they've been left out in the air a few days. She likes her Peeps crispy.

Not me. I'm a gourmand. I like my Peeps chewy and moist. I also like my Peeps yellow.

Peeps started out yellow when they came on the scene almost fifty years ago. They were yellow throughout my childhood. A few were white or pink, but I passed them by. To me, the classic Peep is yellow.

Then, without warning, the folks who produce two million Peeps a day went berserk. They introduced lavender Peeps in '95, blue ones in '98, and this year, strawberry creme. Who ever heard of a strawberry creme Peep? No one. It's unnatural.

It reminds me of the trend a few years ago when pink was all the rage in wedding dresses. That wasn't good, either. Call me reactionary, but a wedding dress should be white and pure, even if the bride is not.

And limousines? Black. Don't argue with me on this. I can't believe they even make white limos, but they do. And poor misguided people ride around in them, no less. Whenever I see a white limousine, I know those inside—often kids going to the prom—have yet to learn the color rules of life.

This becomes even more evident when they emerge wearing powder-blue tuxedos. Tuxedos, like limousines, come in but one color—and if I have to tell you what color that is, you're not paying attention.

Someone started fooling around with pumpkins a few years ago and came up with a white one. I don't know about you, but I don't want a white pumpkin. A pumpkin is about the only thing that looks good in orange. Leave it alone.

Did Lucille Ball decide one day she should be a brunette? No. She knew what worked for her.

It's all quite simple, really. Chocolate should be brown, not white. Fire trucks should be red, not that new phosphorescent green. Ink should be black. Or dark blue. If you get letters addressed to you in red or green ink, throw them out. They're from crazy people.

Shutters on white houses should be dark green. Same for the awnings. Porch ceilings should be sky blue, and the floors should be gray.

When asked about these color rules, my friend Pat added that underwear should be white, nail polish clear, and jeans blue, never black. I agree, although I'm taking her word for it on the clear nail thing.

And since we're rapidly tumbling toward the season, it's not too soon to remind everyone that summer bucks should always be white, but never seen before Memorial Day. As I said, there are rules.

Canadian Geese

Some people say smells bring back the most pleasant memories of their childhood, and I suppose there's something to be said for that.

I can still smell the Sunday roast cooking in the oven when we came through the door from church.

I can still smell the hay in the barn.

And I can still smell the furniture polish that seemed to hang in the air at my grandmother's house. I also can't smell Coppertone without thinking of summer afternoons down at the lake.

But smells are not what bring back my fondest memory from childhood. A sound does. The sound of Canada geese squawking overhead.

My dad used to say we lived directly under the flight pattern for Canada geese, although he always called them Canadian geese. I had no reason to doubt him. At that point in my life, fathers still knew best.

We lived along the shore of Lake Ontario. On a clear night, we could see the lights of Toronto twinkling in the distance.

By my youthful calculations, Canada geese would have *had* to fly over our house, taking into consideration where they were (Canada) and where we were (south of Canada).

Bright boy that I was, I also figured out they had to fly south in the fall in order to fly back north in the spring.

But my memories are not fall memories. They are spring memories, of cool nights and muddy days. Spring was coming. Another western New York winter was almost over.

The geese were telling us so.

My memory is also a night memory. I don't know what the flying habits of Canada geese are, but the geese of my childhood were night fliers. My memory is of lying in bed, listening to their honking above.

They must be talking to each other, I remember thinking. Maybe they were announcing that they could see Canada from where they were—that they were almost home after weeks of flying thousands of miles. Maybe the father, who guards the rear, was telling the mother in the lead that one of the kids was getting out of line.

Or maybe they were just raising hell, heralding their arrival in our neighborhood, telling anyone who would listen that they were back.

Just the other day, a friend of mine was saying that as a child she fell asleep most nights listening to the melancholy wail of a train whistle off in the distance. I felt sorry for her. A train.

I had Canada geese. Boisterous, exuberant Canada geese.

Walking home from work last week, I heard that familiar sound once again. I stopped, looked up, and there they were in all their glory—necks stretched, wings flapping, heading home in perfect V-formation.

"We're back!" they were saying. "Spring is here!"

And for a moment, just a moment, I was back in my narrow bed, falling asleep to their lullaby.

Walking to Work

I walk to work.

When I tell people this, a few are jealous, but most look at me as if I'm some sort of throwback to another era. I suspect some even think there's something un-American about it.

Still, I walk to work. And I walk home. Thirty minutes each way. This summer marks my fifteenth year as a car-free American.

By now, I know every store, every restaurant, and most every face on my route. I know that the windows at Ralph Lauren change every four weeks, and the windows at Eagle Liquor change every four years. I know if I hit the lights just right, I can walk all the way from Washington, D.C., to Virginia without stopping.

Walking has become such a part of my life, I even walk when I'm in Los Angeles, though I wouldn't recommend that for amateurs. Besides, it's very lonely.

Since I live in Washington, where winter is feared more than an independent prosecutor, most people feel sorry for me.

"Don't you hate walking across the bridge in the winter?" they'll ask. I do not. I'm from upstate New York. Winter in Washington, as anyone from upstate New York will tell you, is a joke. Unfortunately, no one who lives here is laughing. It's a town where people carry umbrellas when it snows. Need I say more?

This time of year is another story. July and August. My shirt sticks to my back before I walk a block. The tar sticks to my shoes. I hate the smell of it all.

But we walkers are not complainers. I don't hate it enough to catch a bus or hail a taxi. In fact, I've never taken the bus, and only on the rarest of occasions have I taken a cab. Every now and then a friend will pull over and offer a ride. I decline: It's cheating.

I figure I have walked close to ten thousand miles in fifteen years. The walk has kept me healthy and sane, or as sane as anyone who works at a newspaper can be. We in the business often say we're thankful newspapers exist, since none of us could find work in mainstream society. We're a little quirky. A few of us are certifiable. Maybe walking has kept me from such a diagnosis.

On the bridge I nod to faces I have seen for years. Faces still without names. I see the Georgetown University crew team running back to campus after rowing on the Potomac. They grow younger every year.

And this time of year, I see tourists, maps in hands, their feet sore from a day of sight-seeing, trying to fend off their tired and unhappy children.

Sometimes, if they look pathetically lost or confused, I'll stop and ask if I can help. It's my one-man crusade to dispel the myth that all urban dwellers are mass murderers. This startles them, of course. Some clutch their children closer when I approach.

But after I've told them how to get to the Lincoln Memorial, or where the Kennedys lived before they went to the

White House, or where there's a good place to eat with the kids, they begin to relax.

But I never tell them I'm walking home from work, from another state no less, and that I don't own a car.

No need to scare them further.

Daylight Saving Time

My friend Lisa adores this time of year. Call her a spring chicken, a let's-all-go-outside-and-play kind of gal. She thrives on daylight saving time.

I have no idea why Lisa is my friend.

Even as a kid, when the neighborhood gang would run around in summer's late light until we were all called in for bed, I never liked daylight saving time.

Light was for day. Dark was for night. It was all very simple. I needed order in my world. I still do.

I know I am in the minority. For some reason most people seem to love daylight saving time. Don't ask me why.

The happiest day of the year for me is that last Sunday in October when the clocks go back and darkness falls when it's supposed to. Dinnertime.

I like walking home from work in the dark.

I like settling in for the evening.

I like watching Tom Brokaw without feeling guilty that I'm not outside roasting a pig in a pit or putting together a baseball game with the neighbors down at the park.

Move to Lapland if you want light all the time, that's my bumper sticker. Leave the rest of us alone in the dark.

"Don't you just love the idea you can be outside until

nine?" a woman asked me the other day when the topic of daylight saving time came up at a cocktail party. (You can see how far Washington cocktail parties have deteriorated since Monica left town.)

"No," I said. "I have no desire to be out in my yard until nine."

"But you can do all sorts of things," she said. "You can throw a Frisbee around!"

For some reason, daylight saving time is big with the Frisbee-throwing crowd. Again, I don't know why. As if nine hours of sunlight isn't enough time to throw a plastic saucer through the air. Now they want more.

What's so irritating is that we're supposed to enjoy this added daylight whether we want to or not. There's a sense of obligation about it—get outside and build that Tower of Babel in your lawn! Now!

We're supposed to sit on our stoops and talk to the neighbors.

We're supposed to cook out, grill up a storm, fill the neighborhood with smoke until ten at night.

At times I feel as if I'm supposed to dutifully stand out in the garden until darkness falls before I can go back inside. It doesn't matter that I have nothing to do out there.

We're all supposed to be having fun, damn it!

It's not fun. It's forced frivolity. The whole thing reminds me of those people who run around cruise ships telling everyone the rumba class is about to begin on the lido deck.

Leave me alone! Give me back my night!

My dog, Murphy, agrees with me about this daylight saving thing, and as we all know, dogs are rarely wrong when they sense something's amiss.

Murphy's a woman of routine. She gets up at the same

time every day. She goes to bed at the same time every night. She does not change her routine for this foolishness. (She is also one of those brighter breeds that do not chase anything, so the extra outside time with a Frisbee is lost on her.)

So there she is, poor thing, upstairs on her pillow at 8:00 sharp, trying to go to sleep, as light pours through the window and the neighbors are down below in their gardens, making merry.

She barks at them to keep it down, but to no avail. She is very tired come fall. So am I.

My Grandfather Weaver never played the daylight saving game either.

A farmer, he wasn't going to have the government tell him what to do with his crops, or his clock. He didn't think we were supposed to mess with such a thing. God's time, I think he called it, and he was determined to stand by it. Besides, he was convinced daylight saving time made the chickens act funny.

He was an hour late for everything during the summer months, except for Sunday dinner at our house because my mom would always say dinner was an hour earlier than it was so that he'd arrive on time.

He was a man after my own heart.

Didn't chase Frisbees either.

The Weather Channel

We got cable this year. Yes, we're leaping right into the twentieth century, we are. Just in time, too.

I want to say, right up front, that we did not get cable for the vast variety of programming it offers. We got cable because our TV reception was getting so bad, Katie Couric was standing in a snowstorm most mornings. In July.

So the cable man came and hooked us up. I thought nothing of it. Now I realize I brought a lifetime supply of Chardonnay into the home of an alcoholic.

My partner, Jack, has not left the den. He has become addicted to advancing arctic air masses. He is obsessed with The Weather Channel. Obsessed.

My life has never been filled with such low pressure.

"Violent thunderstorm heading this way!" he'll yell. "Should be here between eight and ten!"

I have no one to blame but myself. I should have seen it coming. When we're on vacation at a place fancy enough for cable, he turns on The Weather Channel the minute he walks into the room.

He says he wants to see if we're going to be on the beach when the eye of the hurricane passes over, or if the clouds that have been hanging over the west coast of Ireland will stay with us for the rest of our vacation.

He also likes to see what the weather is back home, which never ceases to mystify me. If I wanted to know what the weather was back home, I'd have stayed back home rather than spending thousands of dollars to be halfway around the world in the hope the weather would be better.

I'm now convinced that pornography doesn't have as strong a hold on people as The Weather Channel. Jack can watch the various weathermen and weatherwomen parade before the continents of the world for hours.

He watches storms in their infancy.

"Hurricane forming off the coast of Africa!"

He watches the temperature in Minnesota.

"Gary and Sue are getting a cold spell—twenty below!"

He watches the world's hot spots.

"Dubai—a hundred and thirty degrees today!"

I know weather is an obsession for many people. Just not me. I don't even own an outdoor thermometer, something that perplexes my mother no end.

"How do you know what the temperature is?" she always asks.

"I go outside," I reply.

I have come to the conclusion The Weather Channel is really nothing more than an updated, high-tech version of the old Sunday telephone call. The one you got from your parents, who, after concluding you were alive and well and employed, quickly changed the topic of conversation to barometric pressure.

"How's your weather down there?"

"Hot."

"Hot here, too!"

"Supposed to rain Friday."

"Not here. No rain for a week."

This would go on, of course, until all weather fronts had been covered, all precipitation levels measured, all tropical depressions exposed.

The good thing about the "how's the weather" phone call, however, was that it eventually ended.

The Weather Channel, alas, never does.

Early to the Airport

I'm going on vacation in a couple of weeks. I'm flying, and anyone who has flown lately knows I'm in for a few surprises. Delays. Cancellations. Passengers who bite when provoked.

But I know one thing for sure. I know I'll be at the airport early. Very early.

I live with someone who loves to get to the airport hours before the flight leaves. And I mean hours. He would go the night before if he thought the cleaning crew wouldn't disrupt his sleep as he stretched out on one of the benches.

Unlike my friend Katy, who seems to get all her exercise running and jumping on planes just as the door is about to slam in her face, my partner, Jack, likes to get to the gate before our plane even arrives. There are times I wonder whether the plane has even left its previous city by the time we get to the gate to wait for it.

Jack calls it his comfort zone. He reads. He strolls. He talks to the flight attendants who also are waiting for the plane, but I remind him that at least they're getting paid for their time sitting around airports.

Here is his routine:

If our flight is at noon, he wants to be there by ten at the latest.

"You don't know what's going to happen with the morning traffic," he'll say.

If our flight is six at night, he wants to be there by three. If I stall, I can hold him off until three-thirty.

"You just don't know what's going to happen with the afternoon traffic," he'll repeat as he shuffles me out the door.

And if our flight is later—say, an evening flight to Europe—he wants to get to the airport even earlier. He takes the international check-in thing very seriously.

My parents went to England with us a few years ago. We went to the airport at three. My mother was very patient until about five, when she couldn't stand it any longer and asked what time our flight was leaving.

"Seven-thirty," I said.

Jack is not alone. I know there are other airport strollers who like to browse in the shops, buy a newspaper, get some coffee, read *War and Peace* before boarding a plane.

After sixteen years of watching this behavior, I think I have uncovered some kind of "early" gene that exists in his DNA.

While he likes to get to an airport early, Jack also likes to leave concerts early. Get to the car while everyone's still clapping. Get out before the crowds clog the parking lot. Get out before we're stuck in traffic for hours, left with nothing to do but hum over and over again the tunes we just heard onstage. I haven't seen an encore in years.

We left a Tina Turner concert a couple of years ago before she sang "What's Love Got to Do with It?," one of my favorite songs.

As we sped out of the amphitheater's parking lot, I convinced myself that the song was just too old and that she'd dropped it from her show. But at work the next day, a colleague asked if that wasn't the best rendition of "What's Love Got to Do with It?" I'd ever heard Tina do. I lied and said it was.

What was I going to do? Tell him I was home in bed by the time she belted out her thoughts on secondhand emotions?

Thinking back on it now, we left that concert so early, I think Ike was still on the stage with her. I think we left about 1964.

Kid Conversation

I don't talk to people on planes. I'm usually tired, have something to read, and pretty much want to be left alone. And children, of course, are to be avoided at all cost.

So the other morning, on an early flight home from Cincinnati, I wasn't thrilled when a little boy plopped down next to me.

Jeff wasn't thrilled, either. Jeff had to change seats just before takeoff and in the process lost his window position. Great, I thought. Not only am I sitting next to a child, but an unhappy one at that.

But being the bleeding heart I am, I asked if he wanted to switch with me and sit next to the window. It was then I became Jeff's newest best friend.

This was his second flight. His first, from Kansas City, was but a couple of hours earlier. He was with his mother and two younger brothers, on their way to visit a great-aunt.

As the plane raced down the runway, Jeff began telling his life story. He started at the present and worked back, so flying was the first topic. He liked it. He liked being above the clouds. He liked what he called the plane "going sideways." He liked the wings when they bounced.

"Have you ever had a crash?" he asked.

"No, and I'd like to keep it that way," I replied.

"Yes, me, too."

In the next fifty-five minutes I learned more about him than I know about my mother. I learned a few things about myself, too.

Jeff gets five dollars for mowing the lawn back home in rural Kansas. "It's a real big lawn," he says. He now has fifteen dollars in his savings account.

He reached into his back pocket and pulled out a wallet with Old Glory and a bald eagle painted on it. It was attached to his jeans with a long chain. It was quite a wallet.

"For eleven dollars it ought to be! That's why I've got the chain, so I won't lose it." He bought it at Hall's Food Mart in Fort Scott, "a real neat place."

Jeff is ten. He'll be eleven on August 31. In the fall, he'll enter fifth grade and hopes to get either Mrs. Jackson or Mrs. Kirby as his teacher. "It doesn't matter. They're both real nice."

He then asked me why I was writing down what he was saying. I told him I worked for a newspaper, that everyone has a tale to tell and that I liked his spirit.

"Really?" he asked, cocking his head. He then offered me a huge block of pink Bubblicious bubble gum. I declined.

"Bummer," he said. "Total bummeroonie."

Then the questions began.

"Do you know the song 'Shake the Papaya Down'?"

"No, I'm afraid I don't."

He sang a few bars, then asked me what my favorite bird is.

"I don't think I have one."

"Really? I thought everyone had a favorite bird. Mine's the bald eagle. What's your favorite kind of motorcycle?"

I didn't want to tell him that I didn't have one of those,

either, so I said my cousin had a BMW. He wasn't impressed. I knew he wouldn't be.

"My dad used to fix Harley-Davidsons. He died in April."

This last piece of information startled me, in part for the casualness with which it was delivered. I said I was sorry.

"Me, too," he said. "He was a good guy. He could fix anything. I'm kind of like that myself."

He then showed me a photo of his dad, who had died of cancer. "That's where he had to sleep," he said, pointing to a hospital bed.

There was the briefest of pauses, then the conversation picked up again—his three kittens back home, his six dollars in McDonald's coupons, his hope for a tattoo by thirteen, his love of reading. "That's how I know Paris is the City of Light."

At the end of the flight, thinking myself a big shot, I gave Jeff one of my business cards to put in his wallet.

"You forgot the line you're supposed to say," he said.

"What's that?" I asked.

"Here's my card," he said.

So I took my card back and returned it to him with the proper presentation. "Here's my card."

"Thank you very much," he said. "I'll give you a call sometime."

And I have no doubt whatsoever that he will.

Marching Band

When I decided to begin my musical career years ago, I wanted to play the tuba. It didn't matter that I weighed only eighty pounds soaking wet.

I liked the look of the tuba. It was big and shiny and made the kind of noise only a boy could love. I also liked the idea that it was an instrument that could not be ignored. If I couldn't be big, at least my tuba would be.

So the first week of school, I went to Mr. Plummer, the band director, and offered up my services as his newest and most enthusiastic sousaphone player. I could already see myself marching down Main Street on Memorial Day, my tuba gleaming in the sun.

It was not to be.

The rural school I attended had but two tubas, and they had been snatched up by brawnier boys. Mr. Plummer, a man whose life was spent filling gaping holes in his ragtag band, did not miss his chance. He went to the corner of the music room, opened a cupboard, pulled out a saxophone, and handed it to me.

I sat stunned. It was as if I had gone out to buy a tank and come home driving a Chevette. I didn't even tell my parents for days.

A reed instrument. How embarrassing.

But those were the days a student never said no to a teacher, so for six years I played tenor sax in the Lyndonville High School marching band. Okay, let's be honest. I *held* a tenor sax in the Lyndonville High School marching band.

You know the old line about not being able to walk and chew gum at the same time? I could do that. I just couldn't march and play "The Stars and Stripes Forever" at the same time, a shortcoming that frustrated my marching pal and fellow saxophonist, Patty Miller, no end.

"Just play!" she'd say. "March!"

It's not that I didn't want to. I just couldn't.

Mr. Plummer would run alongside the band as it marched up and down the school's parking lot during spring practice sessions, yelling like a drill sergeant at the clarinets, the trumpets, the flutes. And me.

"Are you playing *anything*, Wilson?" he'd yell. "I can't hear a *thing*!"

I nodded my head yes, but my head lied.

But it was worse than that. Forget the song. I couldn't even get my footing.

"Left . . . right . . . left," I would whisper to myself. But after only five paces I always found myself having to skip to get back into step with the rest of the line. It was very clear I marched to a different drummer. Unfortunately, that drummer was not in my school's marching band.

It didn't help that I spent a good portion of my time looking around. During parades I scanned the sidewalks for friends and family. I fear I even waved on occasion.

But I endured. So did Mr. Plummer. And after six years I was actually able to stumble through a rocky rendition of "El Capitán" without my mouthpiece going through the roof of my mouth or my feet tripping the guy in front of me. I think they call such things moral victories.

So to this day I have only the highest regard for any group of human beings who can march to their own music. In step or not. In tune or not. It doesn't matter.

When I see a high school marching band pass me by on Memorial Day, I applaud loud and long, mostly for the kid in there somewhere among the saxophones, whispering quietly to himself.

Left . . . right . . . left.

Prom Night

My niece Laura is going to her prom next weekend.

We had a long-standing pact. If she didn't have a date by prom time, I would fly out to Minnesota and escort her.

It worked.

The thought of going to her senior prom with her fifty-year-old uncle so terrified her, she made sure she had a date, even if she had to rent one.

I'm not saying that's what she did, mind you. I don't know. I'm just saying she made sure she had a date, and she does, with a couple of weeks to spare.

So she's set. She has her dress, her hair appointment, her corsage-bearing escort, if they still do that.

Laura doesn't know it yet, but she's heading toward perhaps the most overrated evening of her life. She won't know that for a while. Then again, she might be the one person in a thousand who has a good time at her prom.

I went to a couple of proms during high school. I have to say I don't remember much about them. Just the usual. The girls spending most of the time in the bathroom, the awkward slow dancing, the parents arriving near midnight to sit in the bleachers and see if their son or daughter would be crowned king or queen of the evening.

I was a prince once, never a king.

But I *was* the decorating chairman for my prom. The theme was "Hawaiian Sunset," and if you don't think that's hard to pull off at the end of a long winter in upstate New York, you've never spent a long winter in upstate New York. It also didn't help that I'd never seen a sunrise in Hawaii, let alone a sunset.

I used my sailboat as the focal point. A fan made the red-and-white-striped sail flutter. Umbrella tables lined the perimeter of the gym, chicken-wire palm trees sprouted from the basketball court, and parachutes hung from the ceiling. Clouds!

I swear you would have thought you were right there on Waikiki Beach, except there was no sand or surf or sun. Instead, there was a rotating color wheel that gave the cinder-block walls, if not the mood of Maui at sunset, at least the ambience of a roadside tavern at Miller Time.

Landauer's department store lent us a battered and bald mannequin from its storeroom. We didn't care that she hadn't seen the light of a store window in years. We stuck her in the trunk of the car, more than happy to give her her day in the sun, or at least her night at the prom.

We dressed her in a grass skirt and halter top and plopped a long black wig on her head. She looked a bit like Cher on a very bad day, which I know now isn't that hard to do. The fact that she had only one hand was disguised by a strategically placed plastic lei.

Maybe I'm biased, but I think it was the best prom ever staged at Lyndonville High School, especially when compared with others that rarely evolved beyond the tired old Kleenex carnation theme.

One was called "Stairway to the Stars." It featured a tinfoil-encrusted staircase leading from center court right up to the backboard. I mean, what was that all about? Not a star in sight.

My niece's prom isn't in the school gym, of course. No one-handed hula girls. No tinfoil stairways. They don't do anything that hokey anymore. Her prom is in a St. Paul hotel ballroom, with dinner at a grown-up restaurant before. And I think I heard something about a limousine.

I'm glad I'm not going now.

Sounds kind of boring to me.

Barbershops

Their names were Mike and Joe, and I'm not sure if they were brothers or not. They might have been.

They were the barbers in town. Everyone went to Mike and Joe. Actually, I went to Mike. My brother went to Joe. Their handiwork cost my parents one dollar a head.

They were right out of central casting. They wore white jackets, the shop had the twirling barber pole by the door, and the magazines were always four months old. *Field & Stream. Look. Boy's Life.* None had covers.

We waited in maroon leatherette chairs with sweeping chrome arms, chairs that bounced if you moved enough, but we weren't allowed to move enough. We sat. And we never talked.

That was for the men who hung out there. I heard a lot at Mike and Joe's, but none of it meant much to me at the time. Town gossip isn't high on a kid's list of interests. All I remember is that the conversation would stop immediately when Mom came to pick us up, a silence that would amuse her no end. I didn't know why then. I do now.

"Men," she would say later, "are much worse gossips than women."

The routine at Mike and Joe's never changed. "Give 'em a

good once-over" was the monthly instruction from Dad. A "good once-over" meant Mike would take the electric clipper to my head and, in less than three minutes, nothing was left standing but a small cowlick up front. The session always ended with a cloud of talcum powder rising from my neck.

It was the same for the back-to-school visit, the Thanksgiving visit, the summer-is-coming visit, although the summer-is-coming visit was even more thorough. I left Mike's chair practically bald every June.

Today I have a lot less hair than I did then, but I pay thirty-five dollars for the privilege of getting rid of it.

Today I go to a woman who has such an exotic name I not only can't pronounce it, I can never remember it. It's something like Myfka. When I call for an appointment, I can identify my "stylist"—that's what they're called now—only by telling the receptionist where her workstation is.

They give out coffee—wine at Christmas!—and all the magazines have their covers but contain nothing I want to read. Or can read. Most are in French, so I look at the pictures.

The chairs are hard. They don't bounce.

But the thing I miss most is the gossip. Now, at an age when I enjoy a good neighborhood scandal as long as it doesn't involve me, I get none for my money. It's all business.

The *process* of getting a haircut is much more elaborate than it was at Mike and Joe's. Now it takes more than half an hour. A dollar a minute, or a dollar a strand, depending on your unit of measure.

When I arrive, a woman who speaks no English wraps me in a plastic cape and takes me into a back room where she washes my hair with exotic-smelling shampoos. She then massages my scalp until I begin moaning so much it scares her, so she quickly wraps my head in a towel and escorts me to my "stylist," whose name I still can't remember.

Then, without fail, the stylist goes into a full-length discussion about my hair's condition and length, as if I were Claudia Schiffer preparing for a photo shoot.

She pulls what hair remains on the top of my head straight up. And looks at it. She pulls the gray hair on my temples straight out. And looks at it.

She's doing this, I'm sure, to make me feel I'm getting my money's worth. It doesn't work.

She wants to talk. I don't.

I can't remember Mike ever talking to me at all, other than his standard farewell when I jumped down off the chair: "There you go, bub!"

I appreciated that, even at a young age. Like a massage, I think, a haircut should be done in silence.

She snips and clips, holding the hair between two fingers. She asks me more questions. Is it short enough on the sides, long enough on top? Do I want to change the part? I always say it's fine, although one of these days I'm going to say, "No, I want it to look like Mel Gibson's hair. Keep working."

Mike never asked me any questions about my hair, in French or English. He never washed it. He never tried to sell me shampoo that would make it fuller. He never held a blow-dryer. He never moussed, unless you call Brylcreem a mousse.

In retrospect, it seems as if he wasn't very interested in my hair at all.

Then again, for a dollar, what could I expect?

From Cradle to Grave

Last Friday I went to a bris for a one-week-old neighbor and a memorial service for a fifty-six-year-old man.

I cried at the first and laughed at the latter.

Maybe that's the way it should be.

Samuel Bennett Bramson is the newest kid on my block, and at noon on a sunny spring day he was surrounded by family and friends who came to be with him for the ancient Jewish rite of circumcision.

His great-grandmother brought her famous brownies and stuffed prunes. His maternal grandfather and paternal grandmother sat by him at the table, while his youngest cousin danced across the kitchen floor until an aunt successfully occupied him with refrigerator magnets.

The father cried introducing his son to the family, which spilled over from the small dining room into the kitchen and up the stairs.

But in no time everyone was laughing over his stories about the legendary grandfather whose name his son now carries.

The baby was then passed across the generations, from mother to grandmothers to great-grandmothers, an act which brought every last one of them to tears.

Ancient phrases were recited. A Hebrew song was sung. Prayers were offered.

And, of course, there was food.

There were so many bagels, and so much kugel, and so much love to go around, that it all overflowed into the garden after the ceremony. Sweet red wine was served in small cups. A toast was made, a life begun.

It was an emotional hour but a grand beginning for Benny, as his parents call him. If the rest of his days are filled with as much joy, I'm not going to worry about him. Besides, he has me for a neighbor. What more could a kid want?

Five hours later, I was sitting in the elegant drawing room of a grand old mansion, listening to people talk about a man I only knew casually.

Gary Blonston, the husband of a friend here at work, was a legend in the newspaper business, a writer's writer, an editor's editor, a newspaperman's newspaperman. He died too young. Cancer.

His daughter talked, halting every now and then for tears. And his father-in-law told tales of a man who had no qualms about doing the Sunday crossword puzzle with a fountain pen, adding that Gary never left the conversation during the process.

Then colleagues from his decades with the Knight-Ridder newspaper chain stood and told stories out of school—stories that caused heads to nod and laughter to roll through the crowd of hardened journalists who have, for better or worse, seen and heard it all.

What they saw in their friend was the best the profession has to offer.

Some of his writings were read aloud. One was a humorous, perfectly paced piece about his attempt to be a cattle-prodding cowboy. Another was but a photo caption describing the pope meeting a young AIDS patient, two or three sentences at most, written with spare elegance.

By the end of the hour-long service, those of us who did not know Gary well wished we had, and those who did sat there with the satisfaction of knowing that someone very special had passed through their lives.

A reception followed. Banquet tables were laden with good food. Scotch and wine flowed. It was a party befitting a man who on more than one occasion was fondly referred to as a bon vivant.

When I left the reception, I told his widow I was ashamed to admit it, but I had had a good time.

She said she was happy about that. That was what Gary would have wanted, she said. A good time.

Both events were a gift that day.

How wonderful to laugh at a memorial service, I thought. To celebrate a life fully lived.

How wonderful to cry at a bris, in anticipation of the same.

The Crying Game

I went to a benefit at the Kennedy Center the other night for an organization called Project Children. It's a great program that brings children from Northern Ireland—both Protestant and Roman Catholic—together for a summer in the United States.

Since it was Project Children's twenty-fifth anniversary, Denis Mulcahy, who founded the organization in his New York City kitchen a quarter century ago, was honored. He was presented with an oil painting, showing him greeting Irish schoolchildren getting off a plane.

When the painting was carried onstage, he stood up in the audience, waved a bit awkwardly, and was given a long and loud standing ovation.

I never met the man. Didn't even know he existed before that evening, but I could have cried. Well, to be honest, I did.

I'm a closet crier. Maybe not so closet.

I can cry at Coke commercials, and I don't even like Coke. For some reason I remember a Coke commercial years ago where the children of the world stood hand in hand on a hilltop singing "I'd like to teach the world to sing."

Don't ask me why, but it always brought me to tears.

I'm a WASP. We WASPs don't cry. I don't know how or

where my genetic flaw occurred, but age is not improving the condition any. If anything, it's getting worse. It's gotten to the point where I cry at farewell parties for people I don't even know.

It happens at both the expected—weddings, funerals, parades—and unexpected times—the grocery store, airplanes, the car wash.

The right song on a car radio can set me off. I was misty-eyed all the way to Boston once during a Judy Collins/James Taylor/Leonard Cohen marathon afternoon. Stone sober, too.

A while ago, my neighbor got married. A man-about-town, he married the nicest woman on earth. "Too nice for you," I told him. He readily agreed.

I had heard the bride's parents were both dead, but I assumed there was a brother, a cousin, an uncle who would walk her down the aisle.

But when I stood up at the church as the organ heralded the bride's entrance, I turned around to find her on the arm of her grandmother. I learned later they were the sole family survivors.

I could weep just thinking about it again. As a matter of fact, I'm tearing up right now.

I bit my lip, looked away, and coughed as the two made their way down the aisle together. I cough a lot when I think I'm about to burst into tears. It's a defense that seems to help.

I cry at movies, too, but at least it's dark. I'm a sucker for the ones that push every cheap button there is. Bette Midler in *Beaches* comes to mind. I can still see her sitting on that beach chair with her soon-to-be-dead friend at her side, the sun going down on the screen and the music soaring through the theater.

Please, don't even bring up *Kramer vs. Kramer.* Last year on a flight from Los Angeles, I read Willie Morris's charming little book about his childhood dog, Skip.

I enjoyed it immensely—I'm a fan of both Willie Morris and dogs—but at the end, there's a poignant scene where Morris sees Skip for the last time. When he pulls away from his parents' home in his car, Morris looks back to see Skip slowly walking over to the curb as if to give his old childhood sidekick one final farewell.

Yes, I'm welling up again.

I closed the book, bit my lip, and whimpered a bit while I looked out the plane's window. Finally, the woman sitting next to me asked if I was okay. Had there been a death in the family? she asked.

I said there had. What was I going to tell her? I was crying for a dog I never knew that died in Mississippi fifty years ago?

Unfortunately, I live with someone who has the same affliction. We can sit on the sofa at night watching *Mad About You* and tear up if we think Murray the dog might be lost.

(Yes, I cried when Mary Tyler Moore turned out the lights of the newsroom years ago.)

Jack is wiser than I am, though. He knows his limits. He knows he can't talk in public, because he'll cry. He always passes when it comes time to give a toast. It doesn't matter the occasion. Farewell party. Wedding. Funeral. Class reunion. Ice-cream social.

He confessed that his eyes filled with tears just the other day at work when he gave an old friend and colleague a promotion. I repeat, it was a promotion.

I've never dared ask what happens when he has to fire someone.

House Karma

I am a firm believer in house karma, good and bad.

For seven years, I lived in a huge old house with a porch that wrapped around my first-floor apartment. There was a fireplace in each room and an antiquated kitchen that boasted linoleum-covered counters and a gas stove that baked everything at 450 degrees.

It was one of the happiest times of my life.

I remember walking into the space, looking around, and telling the landlady, "I'll take it!" This despite the fact I had set $150 as the most I could pay for rent. The apartment was $175.

The windows were floor-to-ceiling, the floors were hardwood, and the bathroom was hospital green, last updated during the war. The Second World War.

The place had good karma. No, it had great karma.

I immediately felt at home there. My furniture fit in perfectly, as did my friends, my family, and the neighborhood dogs that would appear regularly at my screen door for a handout.

Then one day, without warning, new landlords informed me I had to move out in a month. They were not fools. They wanted my apartment.

In a rush, I settled on a place a few blocks away. It was

all wrong. The wood-burning stove was wrong. The modern kitchen was wrong. The karma was beyond bad. I knew it, but I had no choice. I moved in, beginning one of the unhappiest years of my life.

When my partner, Jack, and I went house hunting years ago, we looked for months. Some houses I wouldn't even enter, the karma was so bad. And if I did go inside, I could tell immediately whether I could live there. More often than not, I could not. The lighting was wrong. The "bones" were wrong. The smell was wrong. Instead of welcoming me, these houses were asking me to leave—and I did, gladly.

But when I walked into the town house we have called home for fourteen years, I knew it was the one. We put a bid on it that afternoon. It was ours that night.

A good house is like a good friend. It embraces you every time you walk in. In turn, you accept it with all its quirks and shortcomings. Our house has windows that leak in the winter, plaster walls that crack with the change of seasons, and floors that creak when you cross them. A real estate agent would downplay these things. To me, they're just part of the personality.

My friend Julie moved into a new house this month. She's getting married this spring, starting a new life in new surroundings.

But for almost fifteen years, she lived in a stately old building with thick plaster walls and the scent of floor wax in the air. It not only had character, it had a soul.

When she talked about her old home the other day, a sad smile came to her face. She said the place had treated her well, had been a comforting friend, had given her refuge in good times and bad. It also faced west, giving her years of incredible sunsets.

On her last day there, when the rooms were empty and she was alone, when she was done mopping and sweeping and scrubbing, she said she paused late in the afternoon to watch the sun set one last time.

And tears rolled down her cheeks.

Clutter

At one time or another, we've all been in houses where everything is perfect, right down to the never-been-used guest towels in the bathroom.

I always ask myself the same question when I'm looking around these places.

Where's their *stuff?*

They have things, of course. Beautiful things. Lovely things. Expensive things. And they're all artfully displayed on antique tables and sideboards and handsome mantelpieces.

But they don't seem to have any stuff. The stuff of everyday life.

I was in a perfect house the other day that didn't even have anything on the refrigerator door. Not a dental appointment card. Not a photo. Not a magnet.

The sleek kitchen counters were bare, too. No keys. No sunglasses. No unpaid telephone bill tucked on the shelf over the sink.

They had none of the stuff that makes up the support system for most of our lives.

I grew up in a house filled with stuff. That's probably why I think there's something comforting about having it around. (In defense of mothers everywhere, the presence of stuff does not mean the house is dirty. Stuff is just clutter. There's a big difference.)

Back home, the kitchen counter was the family's depository for everything that came through the door.

At any one time, there was a large selection of my mother's earrings. She always took them off on the way to the bedroom, and she spent a good portion of her life looking for them on the counter when she was ready to head out again.

There were postcards from friends, books from the library, grocery coupons, newspaper clippings on their way to that antique shade of yellow. Stuff.

Throw in some pens, the jar of goldfish food, the hot pad I made at camp, and photos, new and old, waiting for a photo album that never materialized, and you pretty much have an idea of what was around.

When someone asked where something was, the reply was always the same. "It's on the kitchen counter!"

Not that we didn't take some ambitious steps toward tidying up. About once a month, someone would put all the stuff in a neat pile, where it stayed about three hours.

There was also the "string drawer," another one of the family's futile attempts at putting things in order.

You could find most anything in the string drawer, but it was the string that held it all together, literally. All you had to do was pull up on the string and everything else in the drawer came with it. Flashlight, matches, Scotch tape, turkey baster.

Not that stuff can't get you in trouble, mind you. My family still talks of the day the Sunday visitors came.

Back in the days when people took rides on Sunday afternoons, and when people were polite enough to call ahead to ask if they could drop by, a very prim and proper couple from church did just that. They lived in a perfect house where the magazines were fanned out on the coffee table and shoes were never left at the door. I would guess their kitchen counter was bare.

I can still remember overhearing my mother's conversation on the phone. "Oh, this afternoon? Sure. That would be lovely."

She hung up and yelled out that we had an hour to get rid of the stuff. We never mobilized so quickly.

Stuff went flying. Into drawers. Into the washing machine. Under the sink and over the refrigerator.

If the couple had opened any kitchen cupboard, they would have just as likely found my brother's baseball mitt as the cornflakes. Was that a baked potato in the toaster oven or a pair of rolled socks?

I remember thinking at the time: "If these people only knew what was in the dishwasher."

It was an amazing feat, our cleanup effort. But as the couple pulled up in the driveway, we looked around the house and saw that it wasn't ours any longer. The stuff that gave our place a certain patina was gone. To be honest, it felt a bit naked.

I don't remember the actual visit much, but it lingers with us to this day. Mom claims she's still unearthing stuff we buried that Sunday afternoon.

The Garage

My dad was a putterer. That's what he called himself. A putterer. If you ever asked him what he was doing, he'd say, "Just puttering."

He was a farmer. There are no better putterers than farmers. Always in constant motion. Always doing something. Always puttering.

Late in his life, his puttering was confined mainly to his garage. The orchards and barns had been sold off, but the garage near the house remained his domain. It was there he could putter for hours.

My father was not alone. There are millions of men who spend hours puttering in their garages, keeping their own counsel among the rakes and lawn mowers and Maxwell House coffee cans filled with nuts and bolts.

A reader from Chicago called this summer to remind us of that.

He said since it's the one hundredth anniversary of the automobile, that means it's the one hundredth anniversary of the garage, and he was quite emphatic that we shouldn't let such an anniversary go unheralded. After all, what would America be without the garage? he asked.

Indeed. Walt Disney began his empire in a garage. Barbie

got her start in a garage. So did *Reader's Digest*, Buddy Holly, and many a rock band, for better or worse.

My dad didn't invent anything in his garage, other than some Rube Goldberg contraption he came up with to wash the upstairs windows without a ladder. But that doesn't matter. Every garage takes on the personality of its owner. You only have to step into someone's garage and you know immediately who they are.

My dad's garage was neat, but not antiseptic. You couldn't eat off the floor, but the ladder was in the same place for almost fifty years. So was the lawn mower (back right corner) and the birdseed (just to the right of the door).

And above, resting on the beams, were the sleds and toboggan, a collection of pipes that when assembled became a hammock frame, and an old door. The door had been there so long no one knew its origin. Not even Dad.

It was a true garage because it wasn't fancy. It was a plain wood-frame building a few dozen yards from the house. True garages are never attached to the house—their worth always measured by the distance in between.

There are some who believe more marriages have been saved by garages than counselors. They could be right.

Next to being in a hardware store, many a man is happiest when he's in his garage. Alone in the rustic surroundings.

I'm still shocked when I go into friends' suburban (and attached) garages and see finished walls, some even painted. And curtains! Curtains at the window! Who ever heard of such a thing? Curtains in a garage. Certainly not Dad.

Or Howard.

Howard was our neighbor down the road when I was growing up. There were no curtains on his garage windows, but his garage was so clean you could eat off the floor.

The cement was painted high-gloss gray (his car's wheels sat on strategically placed carpet remnants), and even the tools that hung on the Peg-Board over his workbench were outlined in a thin line of paint so when the drill was being used, Howard only had to look up and see right where it needed to be returned.

The garage was his life. Even after dinner he'd return, with his wife this time, to sit at the garage door. Didn't matter that they had acres of lawn to sit on. The garage was the place to be.

I've never quite understood this rural tradition of sitting at the garage door. Maybe it's to get out of the wind. Maybe there's comfort to be found there among the hedge clippers and old license plates nailed to the wall.

Who knows?

Even my parents fell into the habit later in life. They never explained. I'd drive up the driveway on a beautiful day, look out across their vast lawn in search of them, only to find them sitting at the garage door, peering out at the world.

It was a comfort zone.

That's why I've never understood Florida, with its open-air carports.

Where is their comfort zone?

Where do all those men go to be among their things?

Where are their coffee cans of nails?

Where do they putter?

Becoming My Parents

The biggest fear most of us have is that one morning we will wake up and realize we have turned into our parents.

It has already happened to me—twice—and I'm telling you, it can be a shocker.

For years, we watch our parents parade through their lives, doing the most annoying things. Things we vow we will never do. Ever. Then, without warning, it happens.

My first you've-become-your-parent experience came last year. It involved an umbrella.

Umbrellas, as we all know, are fickle things. Like mittens and Donald Trump, they don't stick around for the long haul.

But even knowing that, we went out and bought a nice umbrella. Big, black, beautiful. It would be with us for life.

It was not to be.

I realized this one rainy morning when my partner, Jack, was heading out the door to work, and he pulled one of the old, mangled umbrellas from the stand. I asked him why he didn't take the new one. He then confessed he had already lost it. Left it somewhere. At lunch. At the bank. Didn't matter. It was gone.

And then it happened. He turned to walk away, and the words just flew out of my mouth.

"I'm just *sick* about that umbrella!"

It was my mother speaking, but she was not there. It was a comment that would have irritated me beyond belief as a child. Part chastising. Part guilt trip. Part just a stupid thing a mother would say.

Jack realized what was happening. It scared him. He looked at me, closed the door, and walked away, leaving me standing there in the hallway wearing a pink bathrobe, curlers in my hair, coffee cup in hand. My mother, forty years ago.

It took me a good year to recover from that morning.

The second incident happened just last week. Not as shocking, but alarming nonetheless.

For all his life, my dad puttered around the house. He'd wander up the long driveway, down the long driveway, and across the road to the brush pile. Back and forth he would go with his wheelbarrow, his hoes, his cultivator.

He was very focused on what he was doing, not always aware what was happening around him. He was a farmer, not Mike Wallace.

So whenever a car or pickup would whiz by and a horn would blow, he wouldn't even look up or turn around. Instead, his right arm would just fly up in the air. It was automatic, quick, and, I daresay, a bit disingenuous.

"Who's that?" I would ask.

"Haven't a clue," he would always reply.

I remember thinking how odd that was. Something eccentric people do. Something I would not.

I went home a couple of weeks ago. It was the annual remove-the-storm-windows-for-Mom weekend. I did that, and then I worked around the yard, picking up tree branches from the winter storms, raking off the gravel the snowplows tossed onto the lawn, pulling the dandelions from around the flagpole.

During one of my dozens of trips up and down the driveway to the brush pile, a car went whizzing by as I was heading back up to the house. A horn blew.

Before I knew it, my right arm went flying up in the air, as if being pulled from above. Automatic. Quick. But now I'm not so sure it was disingenuous.

Who was it?

Haven't a clue.

Silent Veteran

My dad was a veteran of World War II, but when I was growing up, he never talked much about his war experiences. It was as if those four years of his life were his alone, something he didn't want to share with any of us. I don't think that was rare among the men of his generation.

He didn't live long enough to see this newfound interest in all things World War II. The flood of best-selling books, the movies about Normandy and Pearl Harbor, the debate about the memorial on the Mall in Washington. It's as if the greatest war of all time has become a cottage industry of sorts.

I'm not sure what he would have thought of all that. Maybe he would have been quietly pleased to think that the men and women who fought the good fight more than fifty years ago were finally getting some recognition.

Then again, he might have found it all a tad embarrassing. He wasn't one to draw attention to himself.

He joined the army the day after Pearl Harbor, left for boot camp in January, married my mom in his uniform one warm day in May, then shipped out for parts unknown in June, not returning home until after the war. Final rank: staff sergeant.

My mother never knew where he was those years he served in the 324th Fighter Group of the U.S. Army Air Corps, but she and Dad devised a code whereby his salutations—"Hi, Honey, Dear June, Hello!"—would pinpoint his general location in the world.

Their letters were so frequent that my mom, now eighty-one, can still remember his serial number, which she wrote on every envelope: 1204449.

He used to say those first years of his marriage were the best. Not one fight.

Over the years, there were a few mentions of chasing Rommel around North Africa and marching up the boot of Italy. And I remember photos of him on a camel at the Pyramids. But that was it.

Then again, as a kid, I didn't ask him about the war. To me, it was already old news, ancient history.

But not to him. Every Memorial Day, after the ceremony at the small war memorial in town, he'd always recite the names of a couple of guys from the county who didn't make it home. The Barnum boys, if I remember correctly. Fighter pilots.

What I remember most are the things he didn't do. He never joined the VFW or the American Legion, for instance. I don't know why. Maybe he felt he'd spent enough time with those men.

He also refused to eat Spam, buy a foreign car, or go camping. Four years in the army was enough roughing it for him, he once said. He didn't need to see the inside of another tent.

That was just fine with me. To a kid, the pool at the Holiday Inn was far more glamorous than any campground in the Adirondacks.

Toward the end of his life, he attended a few reunions of his Army Air Corps group, taking my mother with him to such exotic places as Michigan and Maine.

But as the years passed, the group grew smaller, the trips less frequent.

And then Dad died. Five years ago Saturday. Memorial Day weekend.

Although I certainly didn't think so at the time, in retrospect, his timing was perfect.

Summer

Father's Day

Thirteen years ago this week, I wrote a piece about what to get your dad for Father's Day.

Rereading it the other day, I realized it was filled with uncommon wisdom and that it really ought to be shared with the next generation. It also became very clear to me that I had written much of it with my own father in mind. I don't think I realized that at the time.

My dad died four years ago, but I'd like to think his spirit lives on.

You might recognize someone you know here, too.

—

Rule No. 1: When searching for a Father's Day present, don't be cute. Fathers don't like cute. Fathers don't like surprises, either. If they liked surprises, would they dress exactly the same way every day?

There's nothing more horrifying to a father than opening a present and seeing something he has never seen before. That's why fathers like Old Spice. It's familiar. They know the shape of the bottle, it doesn't have a French name, and no man of questionable sexual orientation has ever worn it.

If you're thinking trendy, don't. This isn't Eccentric Aunt's Day or Cool Brother's Day. It's Father's Day.

Look at his feet. Did he wear the same shoes the day he brought you home from the hospital? Buy him another pair. Obviously, he likes them. Brown wing tips. Maroon Weejuns. Whatever.

What's in his glass? If it's beer, buy him a six-pack of an exotic imported beer. No, wait. Do that only if he drinks exotic imported beers. If he drank Budweiser at your wedding, buy him a case.

Don't get jazzy with the hard liquor, either. If he drinks Dewar's, buy Dewar's. There's nothing sadder than a Dewar's man politely trying to down Chivas Regal, which he can't even pronounce.

Clothing? Steer clear of anything Italian—shoes, pants, coats. Better yet, avoid anything advertised in *GQ.* Have you seen anyone who even vaguely resembles your dad in *GQ?* Of course not.

Fathers own cars. Wash it for him. Coupon books are available at car washes. Yes, it's boring, but fathers are queer for shiny cars. Spring for some wax.

Has your father always read *National Geographic?* Subscribe for another year. Don't give him *Playboy.* He reads it at the barbershop and enjoys it more there than he would at home.

Notepads. God only knows what they write down, but fathers love notepads. Remember how he'd write lists of chores for you to do on Saturdays? You're safe. You don't live there anymore. Give him a stack. He'll go crazy.

Jewelry. Forget it. He already owns a watch. He got a ring when he married your mother. He doesn't want anything else. If he's into open shirts, gold chains, and bracelets, you're on your own. An earring? Don't be funny.

And forget a makeover. The nice thing about fathers is they like themselves just the way they are. Avoid anything that exfoliates. Get real. It's your dad. He still uses Barbasol.

Actually, forget everything I just said. Just call him Sunday. And make him talk to you. No one ever talks to him. When you call home, he always says "Hi," then puts your mom on. Don't let him. Keep him on the line.

You just might learn a thing or two.

Returns

For the first time in my life, I returned something the other day. A garden hose. It fell apart after only a week's use.

Even though the return was legitimate, I still felt odd doing it. We don't return things in my family. You buy it. You keep it. If you've made a mistake, you live with it. You don't complain.

But there I was last Saturday, in one of those huge home centers that seem to have no salespeople, standing in line between a woman holding a lamp ("It was just *all* wrong") and a man holding enough wire to circle the world (I didn't ask).

I didn't have my receipt (we who don't return don't keep receipts), so I sheepishly approached the service counter with the defective hose over my shoulder.

I had my speech all memorized—that I'd bought it just a week before, that while watering the flowers the hose just popped off the spigot, that I thought it shouldn't have happened even if I hadn't bought the top of the line. I was embarrassed and nervous and ready to talk too much.

I got about two words out of my mouth when the clerk interrupted me. "You want to return that hose?" he asked. "Get another one. Aisle Eleven."

"That's it?" I asked.

"That's it," he said. "We take back everything. We've had bathtubs, toilets, kitchen cabinets returned. I don't ask."

My friend Susan, who navigates the shopping world more frequently than I, assured me that returning was just part of the American way of life. You buy. You return.

She even has a name for the phenomenon. She calls it shopping bulimia. You shop, and then you return. You get the high of the purchase and then the cleansing of the return. We regurgitate merchandise.

If anything, I was the odd one, she said.

"You at least had a reason," she says. "Most people have no reason at all for returning things."

We have a mutual friend who returns almost everything she buys. It's sport for her. Her return record is unblemished. Thousands of successful returns.

About the only thing she hasn't returned is her daughter. But it's early. She's only six and a half.

She returned a dining room table after three years. She returned a house once, too, but more on that later.

She's also returned more shoes than Imelda Marcos ever dreamed of owning. Boxes of them. Once she bought ten pairs, and when she returned eight of them a few weeks later, the clerks not only weren't surprised, they greeted her by name.

In area department stores, she's famous. Maybe infamous. Her reputation as the return queen is known far and wide. To her, the right to return is an inalienable one, right up there with the pursuit of happiness.

Shopping bulimia runs in the family. Her mother recently received a letter from Lord & Taylor asking whether something was wrong with their merchandise, since she seemed to be returning so much of it.

But our friend's return of all returns was the house. She bought a house, had buyer's remorse, and even after the inspection and just days before the closing, told her real estate agent she didn't want it anymore and promptly returned it to the bewildered owners. Her reason? She cited disturbing water marks on the wallpaper as if they were stains on a blouse. It worked.

Susan is somewhat amused by this woman, but admits she has to be in the mood to go shopping with her.

"Actually I've never been *shopping* with her," she says. "I've only been *returning* with her."

Maybe it's a male thing, but it has never crossed my mind to buy something on the premise I would probably return it in a week or two.

If I buy a pair of shoes, I take them home and wear them.

If I buy a dining room table, I take it home—and I use the table for the rest of my life.

And once I even bought an old house with water marks on the wallpaper. Kept it, too.

I feel like such a fool.

The Sombrero Syndrome

Americans spend billions of dollars shopping while on vacation. This is not always good. We buy sombreros.

I have done it. You have done it. It's very easy to do.

And you don't have to be in Mexico to buy one. You can buy a sombrero in Japan, in Greece, in Morocco. They are everywhere.

I was clued in to this phenomenon a few years ago when I was in Norway for the Winter Olympics.

I was in a gift shop, looking at one of those huge Scandinavian drinking bowls—the ones that allow you to drink four gallons of beer with two hands and one gulp. My friend Katy came up to me and whispered in my ear.

"Sombrero."

What she was saying was that there are any number of things you can buy on vacation that do not translate once you get them off the plane in Topeka.

I put the drinking bowl back on the shelf.

I did buy a Hawaiian shirt in the Florida Keys once, wore it to dinner there, was quite happy with my black-and-turquoise-floral purchase, and returned home never to wear it again. I was old enough to know Washington wasn't a

Hawaiian-shirt kind of town, but I still succumbed to the sombrero syndrome. It can be strong.

Years ago, my mother and father went to Mexico and brought me an earthenware candlestick with matching globe. The globe had dozens of holes, and each hole was filled with a different-colored marble. When you put a candle inside, you had an earthenware globe that had dozens of holes, each hole filled with a different-colored *glowing* marble.

It was so bad, it was almost good.

"They had them on all the tables at the hotel," my mother said. "It was a big thing in Acapulco."

It was a sombrero in upstate New York.

I feel this is such an important lesson for everyone to learn that I pass on my knowledge to anyone who listens.

On vacation last month in Morocco, I was shopping with some people in my group when I walked up to my newest best friend, Phyllis from White Plains, and whispered in her ear.

"Sombrero."

"What?" she asked, turning to me.

"Sombrero," I replied, explaining the shopping syndrome that has kept tacky tourist shops thriving for centuries.

She looked at the gold-trimmed black caftan with matching head scarf, said, "Oh, my God, it is!" and put it back on the counter as if it were radioactive.

At first Phyllis was not happy with me and her newfound insight into shopping abroad. "I can't look at anything anymore without thinking sombrero!" she lamented at dinner that night.

But then she realized it was like having a sixth sense few people possess. It also saved her a lot of money.

Phyllis grew to like this little game so much that over the next week, whenever someone bought something of, let's say, dubious cross-cultural capabilities, she would just turn to me and stare. She didn't even have to mouth the word.

But sometimes she just couldn't resist.

Sombrero.

Our Italian Adventure

It should be reported up front that no one died. To be more precise, no one was murdered.

In fact, when we parted at the end of two and a half weeks of traveling through Italy together, we were all still speaking to each other. More or less.

When I tell my friends this and declare the trip "fine," they look at me and ask, "Fine? No one was murdered and you're still speaking and you say it was just fine? It's a triumph! A miracle!"

Maybe it was.

Back in the winter, my partner, Jack, and I decided it was time to go back to Tuscany. Drink some wine. Sit in the sun. Visit our friends who conveniently have a little house perched on a hillside midway between Florence and Siena. We also decided to take his twenty-year-old nephew, Kevin, with us. He's about to enter medical school, and this would be a last hurrah for him before a decade without a life.

And for good measure, we asked my seventy-eight-year-old mother to round out the quartet.

Was this mixing of the generations a good idea? Mom remembers World War II fondly, Kevin knows nothing of Vietnam, and Jack and I still think the Beach Boys are danceable. We decide early on never to play the car radio.

Kevin and Mom discover they have more in common than expected. He arrives at the airport with a backpack large enough to stagger Arnold Schwarzenegger. My mother arrives the night before with her closet in tow. She couldn't decide at home, so she brought most everything, waiting to winnow it down to a travel wardrobe at the last minute.

As soon as we arrive in Rome, the generations part. Kevin tries to speak Italian, and Mom attempts to find what she calls "a cup of good old American coffee." Neither succeeds at first, but neither gives up, either. Our fellow travelers are tenacious, if nothing else.

Jack, as usual, is the navigator, missing half the trip because his head is in a map, looking for "interesting" secondary roads. Kevin is the tour guide, able to sniff out a Caravaggio or a chanting monk from miles away, earnestly reading aloud from every guidebook we have.

My mother brings her talent for being able to find a gift shop in the middle of nowhere. (She confesses that once, on a trip to Cancún, she went to the Mayan ruins but never quite saw them when a gift shop appeared at their base.)

On the Rialto Bridge in Venice, I turn around and she's gone . . . lost in the crowd, only to be found in a jewelry shop.

Not that she needs an actual "shop" to shop.

"They call me Grandma!" she proudly announces about her newfound friends, the legion of street vendors who follow her for blocks, imitation designer handbags dangling from their arms. She eventually buys one, not to get rid of them, but because she is so proud she has saved five hundred dollars on the purchase. She refuses to believe it isn't the real thing.

Through all this I am the driver, admittedly playing Mario Andretti on occasion. We scoot through the Chianti countryside, up hills, down hills, shifting as we go. Some would say lurching as we went.

To her credit, my mother screams out only once. Well, twice, but everyone in the car screams the first time, when I pull out from the car rental place in Rome and right into the path of a passing car, which swerves to avoid the crazy American.

Which gets us to the second scream. Our friends who have the house perched on a hillside outside Florence obviously bought the house because of the location. Not only is the view of the Tuscan countryside astounding, so is the approach to the house.

Were the directions written in such a way as to discourage foreign visitors? "After four very tight hairpin turns—keep blowing your horn!—bear off to the left on a dirt road that follows the edge of a cliff."

The road was one car wide, of course, and as I gun up the hillside, I hear noises from the backseat. Mom's trying not to scream but can't hold back. Eventually, she just gives up and throws herself onto Kevin's lap, refusing to witness the exact moment our car will plummet off the cliff and into the olive grove far below.

Mom doesn't know my friends waiting for us at the end of this long dirt road. Priding herself on being put together for any occasion—hair, lipstick, shoes match the bag—she hoped to make a good impression. But when we pull up to the house and my friends come running out to greet us, she is still slumped in the backseat, mumbling incoherently.

At dinner that night, all three hours of it, we eat salads and pastas and Florentine steaks and look out over the countryside as we sip a delicious red wine from tall green bottles bearing no labels. It appears my mother has recovered from the trip up, but appearances can be deceiving.

Our hosts announce that for dessert we are all going *back* down the hill for some late-night ice cream in the village far below.

"No!" my mother blurts out, surprising even herself. "No ice cream!"

I look at her as if she's had a stroke, then realize it isn't the ice cream she's protesting, but the ride down the hill. And in the dark, no less. She didn't come this far to die on an Italian hillside just for an ice-cream cone.

Our Italian hosts seem startled by her vehemence.

"She hates ice cream," I finally say, trying to defuse this potential international incident. "Just *hates* it."

Backseat Bickering

It all came back to me a bit too clearly the other day when I saw two little boys walking down the street in front of me. I knew they were brothers because they couldn't keep their hands off each other.

I followed them for a while, watching them push and shove and kick until one of them fell to the sidewalk with a thud.

"Josh pushed me!" one of the boys screamed.

"Get up!" yelled the mother, who had seen this act before. "Josh! Stop it right now!"

Most parents, unless they have children adopted from another planet, have seen this scene played out a thousand times. My mother still remembers when my brother and I couldn't pass each other without one of us having to hit the other. But if my memory serves me correctly, I think it was always my brother, three years older, who hit *me*, not the other way around. I just want to state that for the record.

I became very good at swerving, ducking, stepping aside. He became very good at anticipating my moves, so contact was made more often than not. For years I had a permanent black-and-blue mark at the top of my arm.

Put brothers in the backseat of a car, of course, and the drama intensifies.

I remember a summer road trip to Santa's Workshop in North Pole, New York. I'm sure my parents felt as if it were a never-ending journey to the real North Pole. My brother and I battled every mile of the way.

Gary had this wonderfully irritating habit of putting one finger over the imaginary line drawn down the middle of the backseat. It drove me nuts, and he knew it. Every few miles, Dad's swinging arm swept over the top of the front seat to calm us down. Mom's swinging arm, while not to be taken lightly, wasn't quite as intimidating.

Once we were heading home, out in the middle of nowhere, and my brother and I were fighting. One of us had crossed the imaginary line for the ten millionth time, and the backseat of our Chevy Impala had become the usual battleground. Mom had had it.

She took her right arm and waved it around in the air behind the front seat in a pathetic attempt to break us up. But with one hand on the steering wheel and the other one flailing around, she looked like a crazy woman waving to someone out the rear window instead of a crazy woman desperate to make contact with one of her boys' heads.

In exasperation, she finally pulled over and told my brother to get out. He could walk home, she said. He could tell she was serious.

But I couldn't believe it when he actually did. He opened the door and just got out, standing defiantly by the side of the road. I can't tell you how victorious I felt, although I have to admit I was impressed with my brother's moxie.

Mom pulled away, and I immediately praised her for her

expert parenting skills, for being so decisive under trying circumstances. I could envision my brother trudging into the house that night, exhausted from his five-mile trek.

But my heart sank when, just a quarter of a mile down the road, Mom pulled into a driveway and turned the car around, heading back toward my brother, who was walking along the road, head unbowed.

"Get in," she said.

He did.

I don't know whom I was more disappointed in.

A Cottage at the Lake

This summer, in one of those slick home magazines that boast page after page of rooms people never live in, there is featured a cottage. They even call it that. A cottage.

But it isn't.

Anyone who has a childhood memory of a summer cottage at the lake or beach knows at a glance that the cottage in the magazine is as far from being a cottage as Beverly Hills is from the Upper Peninsula.

An interior designer has swept through. The rooms are painted shades of pastel blue, the floors are stenciled, and the kitchen shelves are lined with a row of yellow plates all trimmed in blue.

Plates that match? In a cottage at the lake? What a concept! And from what you can see, not a one of them is chipped or cracked.

The place has been raped by good taste.

Summer cottage lovers know, of course, that a cottage can't be gussied up with matching plates or stenciled floors and remain true to the breed. A cottage is not a beach house with all-white furniture, country pine tables, and a state-of-the-art kitchen.

Exactly the opposite. And that's its charm.

To start with, a true cottage is nothing more than a shell. The outside wall is the inside wall. There's no insulation, no wallboard, no painted anything. It's just wood. The floor is almost always covered with linoleum and it's almost always green. Don't know why. Some things just are.

There are several clues that prove the designer "cottage" an impostor.

First of all, there are valuable things in it. There are blue-and-white counterpanes on the beds, some antique sailboats on shelves, and a fleet of white wicker rockers that will be stolen before Thanksgiving if left in any cottage in America during the winter.

There is nothing of value in a real cottage. Ever. And that's what makes it such a priceless commodity in this age of acquisition.

The glasses are jelly jars, the plates are Melmac, the bedspreads are worn chenille, and the art on the wall is nothing more than last year's calendar given out at Christmas by the local oil company.

Furniture? A collection of cast-off chairs and iron beds living out their retirement at the lake. Most everything gets a second chance at the cottage.

The structure itself is an odd collection of two-by-fours and plywood, reminiscent of childhood tree houses brought down to earth. What the cottage carpenter lacks in expertise he makes up for in enthusiasm and imagination. Anyone who has ever walked the floors of a true lake cottage knows it's like walking the halls of an ocean liner during a storm. They rise and fall.

Which is another dead giveaway that the designer cottage in the magazine is no cottage at all. It's too square. It has too many right angles. Someone with a level has been there. An architect maybe? Heaven forbid. If you spill Kool-Aid on the kitchen floor, will it flow out the door? We don't think so.

On Lake Ontario, childhood summers were spent banging the screen doors of dozens of cottages that sat on the bluffs above the lakeshore. They were nothing more than square wood boxes in the winter. But in summer they came to life. Huge pieces of plywood, which acted as practical if inelegant shutters, were raised off the windows by long sticks of wood, turning the cottages into screened boxes that looked like they'd sprouted wings. The summer breeze swept through.

But no matter how much those lake breezes blow, a certain smell always lingers—a mustiness that to any cottage dweller always remains a summer scent.

Even though you went out early in the spring to "open up the cottage," the smell still lingers all summer long—in the corners, the cupboards, the pillows, and the paperbacks that lined the shelf nailed between the beams. The *Reader's Digest* takes on a certain earthiness at the cottage.

The plumbing and the lighting, if they exist at all, are always basic in a cottage.

Often the lighting is nothing more than a lightbulb dangling from a cord. The john is almost always out back.

The real trademark of a cottage, however, is its interior walls. They never go all the way to the ceiling. In truth, there is no ceiling. The walls just end, leaving a black hole where sounds and shadows float in the open rafters above. Voices rise to the beams and bounce back into the bedrooms.

A childhood friend remembers the prime real estate at the cottage was the top bunk bed. From there she could survey the entire cottage—parents playing cards in the kitchen, aunts working jigsaw puzzles in the living room, or, well, you know. . . .

One learned early on that a cottage isn't built for privacy. Then there's the kitchen.

Maybe there's running water. Maybe not. If not, dishes are washed in a huge enamel bowl, the soapy water thrown out onto the lawn by the back door. The counters are covered with Con-Tact paper; the table, an aluminum-legged Formica number with mismatched chairs.

It takes a book of matches to light the stove, and the refrigerator, on its last legs for more than a decade, keeps the milk too warm and the ice too cold. The sole ice cube tray is pried from its narrow, ice-encrusted shelf with a screwdriver.

Looking back at the magazine, the designer "cottage" in contrast has an all-white kitchen with appliances that look like they haven't worked anywhere else before. The fridge even has an ice maker in the door. Where's the fun there?

There's also an indoor bathroom, with a claw-footed bathtub and brass fixtures for the shower and lush towels rolled up in a huge wicker basket next to the tub.

We all know, of course, that real cottages have outdoor showers, which we also all know is the best invention of man. The towels dry on the clothesline slung between the poplars.

Some old friends have such a place in Maine. It is basically a shack, which means it's almost perfect. It's been in the family for decades, and it remains so pure that the matriarch of the clan refuses to even have a dead tree removed from the front yard, even if it is obstructing the magnificent view of Penobscot Bay.

"It's the way it's meant to be," she says.

The cottage has no electricity, no running water, and the bathroom is an ever-moving hole in the ground off in the woods, which as the years advance, we admit, grows less charming with each summer. But it's an honest cottage with linoleum on the floor, no paint on the walls, and no right angles.

Last summer, the family built a new place near the old cottage. The windows are insulated, water actually comes out of the faucet, and the floors are all perfectly flat. The walls even go right up to the ceiling.

In short, everything is wrong.

Screen Door

Every spring, when the weather turns warm, I yearn for a few things I don't have anymore.

I used to have a front porch, for instance, with its robin's-egg-blue ceiling and gray floor and high-back rocking chairs all in a row. I remember I couldn't wait for the first warm day to move everything into place. But I don't have any of that today. I live in a city now, where porches are as rare as clotheslines, something else I used to have.

But last week, when I was going through a real estate open house in my neighborhood—it's one of my favorite Sunday-afternoon pastimes—I came across something I miss even more than a porch.

An old-fashioned screen door.

It was wood, of course, and heavy and painted dark green. It was on the back of a turn-of-the-century house, leading from the kitchen to a small back porch.

It had hung there for generations, its corner brackets still ornately detailed though the paint was a dozen layers thick.

But the best thing about it was the sound it made when I let go of it to walk down the steps and into the garden. Reined in by its tight coil spring, it snapped back into its frame, a summer sound that echoed over the garden walls, down the street, and around the corner.

It was the same sound I heard every afternoon when I came home from school in spring, dashing through the back door and announcing my arrival. Not that I had to say anything. The screen door said it for me.

As spring turned into summer, and the days grew longer, and my gaggle of friends in and out of the house turned into a constant stream, the slamming of the screen door became as familiar a sound as that of the crickets come nightfall.

And I remember my mother's futile effort to stop the cacophony. "Don't slam the screen door!" she'd yell.

But by Memorial Day, she admitted defeat, knowing the banging screen door was to be with her until fall and the arrival of the storm door, which didn't have near the snap.

My aunt and uncle, my grandmother, my grandfather all had screen doors that heralded a visitor's arrival. Everyone did. They didn't even have to look up from the dining room table to know someone was coming through the kitchen.

Even Edna Reimer would stroll out of the back room to see who was there after the screen door announced another milk-and-bread customer at her general store.

Often, the screen was so dark you could barely see through it, and sometimes the frame was so heavy you needed two hands to open it. They were as solid as the houses they hung on.

By comparison, today's doors—with their flimsy tin panels and thin mesh screens—are but sad imitations, the sound they make as hollow as their innards.

I didn't buy the house the other day. I wasn't in the market for a million-dollar home in need of repair.

But I did tell the real estate agent on the way out that the next time he lists a house's selling points, he should place a perfectly aged screen door right up there with the Sub-Zero refrigerator, Corian counters, and gas-burning fireplaces.

And, yes, he looked at me as if I had lost my mind.

In Praise of Porches

The apartment had big rooms. Handsome tall windows. Hardwood floors. A fireplace. The fact it rented for $175 a month made it even more appealing.

But what sold me on the place was the porch—a wide, wonderful porch that wrapped itself around two of the apartment's three rooms. It could easily hold a hundred people, and did, on more than one occasion. It was a grand promenade, and it was to become my summer haunt for almost a decade.

There are special places we remember from our summers past. A family cottage. A row-house stoop. Maybe an ice-cream stand on the edge of town. Mine is that porch on Caroline Street in Saratoga Springs, New York.

The huge Queen Anne house had porches galore. First floor. Second floor. Third floor. They were everywhere. It seemed every room opened onto a porch.

It may sound simplistic, but America would be a better place if there were more porches. There are too many decks today. Too many patios. Too many glassed-in "Florida rooms." Just saying "Florida room" makes me cringe. All are in the back of houses. All are antisocial. All separate people from their neighbors and passersby. You need an invitation to get into them.

Only porches bring people together. Only porches say "It's okay to come up and sit."

The front porch—that everyman's land between inside and outside—is better than either. You're covered from the elements, but not surrounded by walls. You're exposed, yet protected.

"Halfway inside the house and halfway outside, the very ambiguity of the front porch has encouraged a variety of interpretations and uses over the years," writes Akiko Bush in the current issue of *Metropolis* magazine. "Most of these have to do with casual interaction among people, indicating that the front porch's social function is as important as its architectural definition."

Shortly after I moved into that apartment on a winter's day almost twenty years ago, I picked up four rocking chairs at a barn sale. They had wide woven seats and high backs. They were bright green, the color of early summer.

When spring came, the fern and ficus moved out to the porch for their annual airing. A couple of worn Oriental rugs were scattered on the floor. I lined the four rocking chairs up in a row, Grand Hotel style.

The porch was open for business. It wouldn't close until way into October.

A porch is really a stage, and this one was mine. I gladly shared it.

A friend would sometimes bring her cello over and give open-air concerts. My mother's sixtieth-birthday party was on the porch. Fifty people came. Some I didn't even know. Strangers saw a good time, came across the lawn and up the stairs. I offered them a drink and they accepted. In return they kissed my mother. A fair deal.

Almost every house on Caroline Street was built before the

turn of the century, so almost every house on the street has a porch. The Collinses across the street had a porch. So did the O'Donnells. The O'Donnells were world-class porch sitters.

Even the Serlings, who built a new house on the vacant lot next door, were wise enough to hire an architect who gave them a house with steep gables and three porches.

One summer we formed the Caroline Street Porch Sitters Association. It wasn't as idyllic as it sounds. It turned into a cutthroat competition to see who could put in the most hours of porch sitting.

The O'Donnells won, but I did give them a good run for their rockers. Sometimes we'd stare each other down across Caroline Street, hoping someone would give in and go to bed, leaving the other the victor for at least that evening.

But more often than not we'd be lured to one another's porch for a drink, a chat, some neighborhood gossip.

We'd watch fireflies together from the porch. We'd sit in silence and watch a summer storm pass through.

And late on August afternoons when the long shadows fell across the lawn, we'd watch the railbirds stroll back from the racetrack, their daily programs folded and stuffed in their back pockets—winners and losers heading down Caroline Street to the bars.

The races are on in Saratoga Springs again, and the grand, palm-filled porches along Union Avenue and North Broadway—maybe even my old porch—are filled with the sound of laughter and the tinkle of glasses. Even if you just pass by, a broad lawn away, you have to smile, knowing once again a porch is working its magic.

People say porches are making a comeback. I would be happy if I thought it were true, but I don't. Some of the pseudo-Victorian, aluminum-sided monstrosities springing up in suburbia these days have porches, but many of their porches are just decorative—often not wide enough to even put a chair on. And if you could, what are you going to see if you sit out there? People don't walk by in suburbia. Why would they? There is no place to go.

One of my dreams is to someday have enough money to hire an architect to build a house. It would have a porch as wide and welcoming as the one on Caroline Street.

The architect would even measure me to make sure the railing was just the right height for my feet to rest on when I sat in a rocking chair. Once the porch blueprint was done, the architect could do anything he or she wanted inside. I wouldn't care.

It's the porch that matters.

I don't know who is living in my old apartment these days. I hope it's someone who appreciates a good porch. As for me, I live in a city town house now. I have a brick-walled garden covered with ivy. When I entertain, I roll out one of the old Oriental rugs for old times' sake.

People tell me it's lovely. But I know the truth. It's no porch.

Adirondack Chairs

We bought an Adirondack chair at Smith & Hawken the other day. It's grand, with its trademark fanned back and sloping seat and broad arms. It's guaranteed to take us far into our retirement years. The saleswoman told us so.

Actually, it's a rocker, which real Adirondack chairs are not. It was a compromise. I wanted a stationary Adirondack chair. To me, that's the whole point. You're not going anywhere when you lower yourself into one of these classics. But my partner, Jack, wanted the rocking version.

There are things to argue about in this world. Adirondack chairs are not one of them. So we carried it home by its sturdy arms. It now sits in our garden.

I don't know who came up with the idea for the low-slung original with arms so wide they can hold a book and a drink and whatever else you might happen to need on a sunny afternoon. Whoever it was, that person should be awarded the Nobel Prize for seating.

Most chairs these days are boring. Utilitarian at best. And more often than not, they're as uncomfortable as hell. I was at a dinner party the other night where the chairs were so poorly designed that I wanted to go home before dessert— and I never want to go home before dessert.

At times, I think chair designers are a sadistic little lot, perhaps getting back at the world for those hard chairs we all had to sit on back in Mrs. Bane's second-grade class. And don't even get me going on those wood planks that pass for pews in Methodist churches.

So imagine a chair that actually beckons you.

Come.

Sit down.

Bring an afternoon's reading.

Bring some iced tea.

No, bring some wine!

Stay awhile.

Fall asleep if you like.

I remember a row of Adirondack chairs sitting on a bluff in front of my Uncle Bud's cottage. The adults sat and talked as we kids romped on the stony shore below. At the time, I wouldn't have changed places with them for anything in the world. Now I realize they had the best seats in the house.

A couple of summers ago, I was visiting my old friends Pam and Tom in Maine. They live in one of those glorious houses, the kind not built anymore—gables galore, a porte cochere, and an endless porch lined with rocking chairs. But best of all, out on the lawn, between outcroppings of rock, sits a weathered Adirondack chair facing the sea.

Whenever I'm there, it calls to me. That visit was no exception. I dragged it to a sunny part of the lawn and settled in for an afternoon with some old *New Yorkers*. Before long, I had fallen asleep in the sun, a happy man in the arms of his Adirondack chair.

Pam drove up the long driveway and saw me slouched over, my chin and magazine resting on my chest. Could I have been drooling? Perhaps. She said she stared at me for a moment but decided to leave me alone.

She must have thought it looked like a scene out of *Cocoon*, because when I finally awoke and went in the house, she said but one thing. There was a certain sadness in her voice. "Oh, we've all gotten so old," she sighed.

For some reason, that news didn't sound so bad.

Clotheslines

I know you don't see them much anymore, and I know the better social circles wouldn't be caught dead with one in their backyard, and I know there are even strict ordinances against them in the most common of subdivisions now. But I don't care.

It's summer. I want a clothesline.

I want to walk across a lawn with a basket of wet laundry in my hands, fumble around in a bag of wooden pins, and hang up clothes. Out of my way. I'm moving down the line.

I grew up with a clothesline right outside the kitchen window—two lines strung between T-shape metal poles. As soon as I was tall enough, my mom taught me how to hang clothes. Yes, there is a method. Towels with towels. Sheets with sheets. Shirts all in a row, held together with but a single clothespin between them.

We were a wood slip-on clothespin family. We didn't do those with the spring action, and never the plastic variety, but I guess it's all a matter of personal taste.

All clotheslines are not created equal, either. I don't understand those smaller four-sided ones, for instance. The ones that rotate on one pole. They aren't real clotheslines. They're too confined. Too restrained.

Real clotheslines are long and elegant, a simple straight line that allows the wind to work its wonders.

There was no shame in having a clothesline when I was growing up. There was nothing low-rent about it.

If anything, there was a bit of competition in rural upstate New York when it came to hanging clothes. I remember riding the bus to school and passing clothesline after clothesline filled with the daily wash, one more beautiful than the other.

Clothes hanging is a work of art. Done properly, it can put a Calder to shame. It takes on a life of its own. Shirts shudder. Pants dance. Towels flap and snap.

But it is the broad white sheet that is the king of the line. Watching them whipping in the wind is akin to watching the flag go by on the Fourth of July. It can bring a tear to the eye.

I have been known to pull over on a country road if I see a clothesline of sheets in full sail.

And the smell! Let me die with my face in a sheet that's been hanging on a clothesline all afternoon.

What's that, you say? Did I hear you say I'm strange?

Well, if you think I'm odd for saying I love burying my face in a crisp, cool sheet right off the line, then you've never buried your face in a crisp, cool sheet right off the line. Your loss. I have no idea why people take drugs when there are fresh-off-the-clothesline sheets to sniff. A lot cheaper, too. And it's legal!

Take them down, put them on the bed, and you have one great night's sleep ahead of you.

There's a laundry product out today that boasts it can make clothing "clothesline fresh." Just pop it in the dryer. Whom are they kidding? Not me. And not anyone who has ever had the privilege of owning a clothesline.

I love summer cottages because they always come with a

clothesline, often strung between two trees. In the morning, the bedding billows in the wind off the lake. In the evening, the beach towels snap to attention, right alongside the bathing suits from the afternoon swim and the dish towels from dinner's washup.

I bought my first house for two reasons: a front porch and a clothesline. The clothesline ran from the back kitchen door out to the corner of the barn. It was on a pulley. I could stand in one place and hang all the clothes, pulling them toward the barn, where they were eventually high enough to catch the wind.

It was better than hoisting a sail.

I'd do a load of clothes before I went to work in the morning, hang them up on my way out the door, and arrive home at night to the best-smelling wash in Saratoga Springs, New York. From April to November, I never used my dryer. It was heaven on earth.

And the *real* heaven? I'd be sitting in a dark-green rocker on a wide front porch. In one direction would be a perfectly stacked wall of firewood as far as the eye could see. And in the other? The longest clothesline imaginable, filled with nothing but miles and miles of white sheets billowing in the wind, putting the clouds to shame.

Outdoor Showers

If you've never owned or rented a cottage at the lake, or a beach house at the shore, you wouldn't understand. But if you have, you already know the pleasures of the outdoor shower.

It sounds like such a simple thing, an outdoor shower, but in fact it's one of mankind's greatest inventions.

Where else can you stand before all creation, under an open sky, shower the sea's salt from your skin, and do it all behind nothing more than a bush or a hedge or a teetering screen of latticework built by some weekend carpenter who should never think of quitting his day job?

I remember well the first time I showered au naturel outside. It was at a cottage on the sandy Canadian shores of Lake Erie. I remember standing on a wood pallet, turning the faucet on the side of the cottage and screaming as cold water sprinkled down on me from the oversize shower head above. And all without a bathing suit on, no less!

It was heaven.

I felt a little decadent, although I didn't know what decadent was at the time. I was ten. All I knew was I liked it. It was like sleeping without pajamas, although I didn't know that pleasure yet, either.

There are far too few activities left in life that allow you to wear no clothes outside. Legal activities, anyway.

Over the years I've vacationed at beach houses from Maine to Miami, and the first thing I do is look to see if there's a shower tucked away somewhere, hanging off the side of the house or behind a boxwood hedge. If not, it's not really a beach vacation.

I mean, what's the point? You drive for hours to get there, you unload a trunk full of groceries and clothes, you rush to spend that first afternoon at the beach, and then you get back to the house and have to shower inside? Doesn't seem worth the effort to me.

Some would say you should go inside to shower, but some would be wrong. I'm sure it's only a matter of time before a do-gooder will come along and attempt to ban outdoor showering. Of course, this will be someone who has never taken an outdoor shower but heard somewhere along the way that it's a pleasurable, enjoyable, liberating activity, and therefore potentially hazardous to the family unit.

We will fight them to the end!

We will fling bars of Ivory soap if we must!

The Society for Outdoor Showering (SOS) will mobilize!

But let's be rational about this. If anything, showering outdoors is as wholesome as singing in the rain. Except you have no clothes on. How can you argue against cleanliness? How can you argue against no sand in the house? The whole operation is a perfect exercise in efficiency.

After a long day at the beach, your skin still tingling with the sun, the salt still on your lips, you step behind the hedge, turn on the tap, and let the water run down your tan line. You wash the sand out of your hair. You wash the sand out of your swimsuit. You wash the sand out of your day.

Only then are you ready for cocktails on the porch, a beach activity that also has its charms. But it's no outdoor shower.

Camping

All of my friends have sent their kids to summer camp.

As far as I can tell, this is good for the kids and great for my friends. I am beginning to understand that camp was invented for the parent, not the child. I am a slow learner.

These days, it seems, kids go off for weeks, or even months, at a time. No one-week sojourns for them. There's ballet camp in the Berkshires, computer camp in the Poconos, soccer in Michigan, horseback riding in Virginia, surfing in California.

No child just makes lanyards anymore.

Not that I'm a big lanyard fan. I am not. Had to make one once and remember asking myself at the time why. I came up with no good answer.

And when the crafts counselor came out with the Popsicle sticks and glue and began showing us how to make a jewelry box, I knew we were going down a path I had no intention of wandering. When she announced the box's feet would be pieces of macaroni, I stopped construction immediately.

I had my standards, even back then.

I was never a happy camper. Only went twice. Hated it each time. No, you don't understand. I mean hated it.

Maybe not as much as my friend Ron, who rolled in poison ivy just so he could get sent home—it worked—but I hated it just the same. I just wasn't as creative as he was.

No one was more homesick at camp than I was, and I was only gone for a week. If I could have climbed back into my parents' Chevy Impala and returned home with them that first day, I would have. But they seemed determined to give me the camp experience. They left me holding the duffel bag.

Why leave my dog, my room, the farm to sleep with a bunch of strangers in a cabin that smelled of something I had never smelled—before or since? Why stand in line to brush your teeth? Was this supposed to be fun?

I even sent my parents a postcard telling them how I was crying while I was writing it, hoping they'd jump into the car and come get me. It didn't work. They got it after I got home.

And then there were the counselors. Two of mine were so nurturing they took a group of us up on the mountainside, sat us around the proverbial campfire, had us sing songs, then quietly disappeared into the dark woods to make bear noises behind our backs.

Never ran so fast in my whole life.

That did it for me. Haven't camped since. I don't own a tent, don't own a sleeping bag, and I have no desire to sit on a rock and sing "Kumbaya." Sitting on a porch is as outdoors as I want to get on a summer's night.

I don't even understand the RV phenomenon. Why do millions of Americans want to drive down the highway with a tea kettle jangling on the stove behind them, only to pull into some campsite at night and turn on the TV?

I mean, if you're going to camp, camp. Otherwise, stay home, where at least your stove stands still.

As for me, give me a hotel with plush towels and great soap and nice cotton sheets, and I'll set up camp with no protest. Roughing it is when the tub comes without a Jacuzzi.

Sweet Corn

August has nothing to recommend it except one thing. Fresh sweet corn.

It almost makes the month bearable. Actually, it does make the month bearable.

A pot of boiling water, a dozen ears of corn, a pound of butter, five minutes of your time, and you have yourself the best meal on earth.

Which brings me to my friend Barbara. Every August I think of her because she loves corn on the cob more than I do, if that's possible.

Barbara eats her sweet corn with such wild abandon, with such relish, with such enthusiasm, that when she puts down that last cob, buttery kernels stick to her cheeks, and little pieces of yellow are sprinkled through her hair.

I remember always being startled by how she would look after a round with a few ears, but, busy eating my own corn, I never looked up long enough to see how she got herself in such a state. Friends tend to overlook many things.

Barbara, pro that she is, eats sweet corn with incredible efficiency. A retired newspaperwoman, she acts as if she's just writing another deadline story on her old Royal typewriter. Except this time it's with her teeth.

When she gets to the end of the cob, she immediately swings her head back to the left and starts over. She goes through an ear of sweet corn quicker than she can type. And she can type.

I'm not quite as fast, but I'm no slouch, either. Do I stop when I get to the end of a row? Do I set the corn down and eat something else on my plate in between? Do I come up for air? No. I keep right on.

I couldn't care less what else is on the plate, what the conversation is, who my dinner partners are. One of my big fears is that one day I'll get invited to dinner at the White House, and Hillary will serve sweet corn and I won't remember a thing.

One ear. Two ears. Three ears. I can't stop. If there were a twelve-step program for sweet-corn eaters, I'd be a prime candidate for admission. I admit I am powerless over the stuff, that my life becomes unmanageable in August.

I was at a farm stand the other day, counting ears of sweet corn into a paper bag. I was going to buy one dozen. I bought two. Could have bought four.

I won't tell you how many ears of corn I've eaten in one sitting. Even I have some pride left. But it's more than six. Way more.

Only when the season is over can I eat vegetables with any kind of detachment.

Oh, peas! How nice.

Carrots? Lovely. Yes, I'll have a few.

Sweet corn? Don't get me started.

We sweet-corn aficionados know there is only one way to eat it. The way Barbara and I do. Down the rows from left to right in one rapid motion. No stopping. Then repeat.

But the other day I had dinner with an old friend who

picked up her corn and started eating it in circles, around the cob, not down the row.

Can you imagine? I'd never seen anything like it. I'm not sure I like her anymore. It was like finding out she was a Republican or something.

Not only that, she stopped and talked while eating, as if the corn weren't the most important thing in her life at the moment. She treated it as if it were something she could put down if she had to. Barbara wouldn't have understood. I certainly didn't.

When I questioned her about her corn-eating habits, she acted as if I had chastised her for using the wrong fork for the salad. She got defensive. In the interest of friendship, we dropped it, but to be honest, I'm not sure I'll see her again. There are eccentrics, and then there are eccentrics.

She even used those corncob holders. What a sissy.

But more disturbing than her behavior was that of a man who casually told me last week, at a sweet-corn-filled picnic no less, that he didn't like the stuff. Only ate it once. Said it was too messy.

He didn't like eating with his hands, didn't like the butter running down his arms, didn't like the way it stuck between his teeth, didn't even particularly like the taste.

I slowly backed away. I know the rantings of an unstable man when I hear them.

Summer Tans

It's the end of August, and once again I have failed. I have what can only be described as a mediocre tan.

I know, I know. I'm not supposed to get a tan anymore, so save your phone calls, your e-mail, your letters. I know getting a tan is not good for me. I try to be good, but it's hard. I love the sun.

We all have to die of something, and you might as well look good on the way out. That's my theory. Nothing worse than a lily-white corpse.

That's why I've never understood smoking. You only get brown on the inside. And then you die. But by tanning, you get the most beautiful brown on the outside, making you look like the healthiest person alive. You're not, of course, but it's all in the packaging.

I come from a long line of tanners. My mother, in shorts and halter top, used to drag her ironing board outside and plug into the garage socket just so she could iron under the sun. She was as brown as a berry by the end of August. Still with us, too.

My dad used to be dark as molasses this time of year, too, although I have to admit it wasn't always attractive. He would get what's called a farmer's tan. You know, tanned arms, tanned head, tanned neck, white body. Not pretty.

But he looked great as long as he kept his clothes on, which he managed to do most of the time.

As for me, I was out in the sun for hours. I'd work in the orchards, go swimming down at the lake, run around the yard in the noonday sun, all without a drop of suntan lotion on my body. Never thought a thing about it.

My tanning obsession got worse as I got older. I remember college trips to Florida, where we'd sit on the beach for hours, slathering ourselves with baby oil every ten minutes. No SPF 30 for us. I'm not sure SPF 30 even existed back then.

Just put on the oil, recline, fry.

One friend hung out the window of the car on the way back north in a gallant effort to keep her tan going as long as she could. That brown skin was a badge of honor.

I even owned one of those folding cardboard reflectors, the ones you held up to your face to pull in the sun's rays. It came out whenever sunshine appeared in upstate New York in March.

Those days are long gone, of course. The skin-cancer police are everywhere now, asking if we don't have a hat we could put on, a blanket to cover our shoulders, a sunscreen with a higher number than our age.

Even when I sit on a park bench for five minutes now, my head tilted back toward the sun, people walk by and stare at me as if I have some kind of a death wish. Maybe I do.

My only hope is that they lay me out in a starched white shirt—better to show off a fabulous tan.

White Bucks

I have owned a pair of white bucks for years now. They're a bit battered, not quite as white as they used to be, more cream color these days than anything else.

The pink soles are worn at the heels, and there are a couple of pretty bad scuffs at the toes, scuffs that can barely be disguised any longer by the white powder I rub on them every few days. But it doesn't matter. I like them just the way they are.

They're like old friends who come to visit every summer, friends who grow more comfortable with the years.

They appear on Memorial Day and know enough to disappear that first weekend in September. They wouldn't think of staying longer. They know the rules.

My dad always used to say you can judge a man by his shoes. He wasn't talking about white bucks, of course. He was talking about highly polished wing tips. But I agree.

When I see another man wearing white bucks, I instantly like him. Especially if he's of a certain age. Without even walking across the room to speak, I know he has a good spirit about him, a spirit that doesn't come with those sensible black lace-ups worn by publishers, politicians, and priests.

I also know his white bucks will not be new. I know the two have been together for many a summer.

I can see the garden parties they have walked into, the afternoons they have spent at the track, the gray-painted porches they have strolled across on their way to another martini on the rocks, perhaps with a twist, perhaps not.

To some, I'm sure we white-buck wearers look like the Good Humor man or a stray member from Professor Harold Hill's marching band. Others, I'm equally sure, would say there's a certain affectation that comes with wearing white bucks, but they would be wrong. They're just a little madcap, that's all, a shoe that proves even your feet can have fun every now and then.

GQ this month, pushing brown-and-white spectators as the newest best thing for men's feet, was rather cruel when talking about white bucks in a dissertation on summer style. The writer said they can give the impression of an off-duty hospital orderly. I suppose that's true if you walk around in them with a thermometer and a clipboard, asking people how they're feeling.

But we white-buck wearers are used to such swipes. On occasion, someone will call me Pat Boone. I've been called worse. Believe me. And sometimes they will say nothing at all, but I can tell what they're thinking. *So who is this dandy?* But at a party the other evening, for some inexplicable reason, a number of people came up and complimented me on my white bucks.

"I don't know why, but they always make me smile," said one woman.

When was the last time your Doc Martens did that?

A Dog in Summer

Next time around, I want to come back as a dog. Preferably in summer. Actually, I'd be happy to come back as a dog any time of year, but summer seems to offer the best opportunities.

Sleeping on grass.

Hanging out with the guys.

Snatching a steak off the grill.

Does it get any better than that? I don't think so. And you certainly don't hear any dogs complaining.

Nothing is planned in a dog's summer. The world is their biscuit. Everything is spontaneous, life a constant adventure. And the best part of all is you get to do it barefoot, grass under your four paws, sand between your claws.

I can see me now, sticking my head out the car window, nose held high in the air, ears swept back, eyes scanning the horizon. I watched a dog in that regal pose just the other day, his paws firmly planted on the window frame as he sped by. He looked beyond happy, his expression closer to bliss.

"Faster!" he was saying to his chauffeur. "Faster!" As if he had some place to go.

Oh, to be a dog in summer.

Let's chase a few cars, flirt with the poodles in the park, lick ice cream from some kid's cone, if for no other reason than to teach him the importance of sharing.

And if we have time, we'll torment the cat next door. The one who smugly sits in her kitchen window behind the screen, the one who thinks she's smarter than everyone else, the one who needs to be put in her place.

But enough about her. We have better things to do. Like dancing in streams, snapping at bees, howling like a fool at the August moon. It's all about expressing oneself, this being a dog in summer.

We'll stand guard at the end of the dock; we'll go swimming with the gang; we'll paddle in circles till we're dizzy. Then we'll lounge away the afternoon on the porch.

But not before we shake the water from our backs, spraying the crowd, making them shriek with delight. It's the best thing about being a dog in summer.

Maybe we'll chase a stick or two. Maybe even a Frisbee. But only on our terms. The weather has to be just right, the rewards determined ahead of time. Sometimes humans need to be reminded that these foolish games are for their amusement, not ours. There will be no stupid pet tricks. Not from us. Not this summer.

We are not fools, we dogs of summer.

When it's a hundred degrees in the shade and we're dragged outside, we'll sit without being told. There will be no budging, not until it's clear the movement is back toward the house, back to where it's cool, back to where there's water and a cookie jar of treats on the kitchen counter.

And then we'll jump onto our favorite chair, the one under the air-conditioning vent, rest our chins on its arm, and drift off to sleep, dreaming of falling leaves and cool nights, longer walks and shorter days, the coming pleasures of fall.

As I said, we'll happily be a dog for all seasons.

This Old House

The farmhouse my great-grandparents built at the turn of the century in upstate New York passed out of the family this month. It was bought by a man I do not know.

Family legend has it that my great-grandfather was furious at the builders when the final price tag in 1901 came in at $3,900, double the initial estimate.

But for that price, he got a house so big, so tall, and so massive that painters sometimes balked at taking on the job of giving it a fresh coat of white.

By the time I arrived on the scene, it was home to my grandmother, my aunt and uncle, and my cousins. Just up the road, a five-minute walk away, it was my second home.

It never crossed my mind growing up that one day a Wilson wouldn't live there anymore. After all, my dad was born in an upstairs bedroom. His grandfather and father were laid out in the front parlor, the same room where we celebrated Christmas Eve every year. But as a kid, you never think that times change, that people move on, that very often life offers up circumstances beyond anyone's control.

Most of us of a certain age have such a place in our pasts. Usually a grandparent's house, the kind not built anymore.

Big, with heavy storm windows that had to be removed in the spring, and wood screen doors that banged with every coming and going on a hot summer's day.

Architecturally, the house was an elephant. Lumbering, ponderous, yet somehow comforting. The attic was bigger than most people's homes, and there were so many rooms upstairs, an inquisitive child could spend years exploring them, and did.

There were front stairs off the living room and back stairs off the kitchen and steep stairs to the cool stone-walled cellar where rainwater was collected in a cistern. And there were porches—front, back, and side. There even was a porch off a bedroom upstairs; it could be reached only by climbing out the window.

There was a front door, too, but it was knocked on only by traveling salesmen. Everyone else came in through the kitchen, where plants filled the windows.

Not that the place didn't have its eccentricities. A downstairs bathroom was so cold, you never lingered long in the winter, and the water pressure in the upstairs bathroom was so poor that you couldn't shower. The shower was in the cellar, used by my uncle and cousin when they came in from the orchards.

There was a huge wood-paneled pantry, and a glass-door kitchen cupboard that went right through to the dining room, a feature I thought quite inventive at the time.

And then there were the smells. Glorious smells.

The kitchen during canning season, when applesauce was strained through an old metal sieve; the mudroom in winter, when it reeked of wet wool; the stairway to my grandmother's quarters, where the scent of furniture polish mingled with that of fresh chocolate chip cookies and the faint smell of the perfume she always wore.

Gone, yes, along with the house.

But very much still here.

Vicki's Funeral

An old college friend died this month. She was forty-nine. Yes, too young.

Vicki was a character of the first order, a woman who never ceased to both amuse and amaze. Bigger than life, as they say. Whenever I needed a pick-me-up, she was excellent tonic, and for thirty years she'd always been there for a laugh or two.

Our lives had taken various twists and turns since college, but we both landed on our feet by middle age, a bit battered but not broken. We liked to think we were just hitting our stride.

So when the call came that she had died of congestive heart failure, it seemed surreal, and more than a bit unfair.

But, yes, I told her daughter, I would come to the memorial service. Of course.

Would I like to say anything at it? she asked. I think I would, I said. I didn't share with her my bigger concern: Could I?

A few days later, I flew north, rented a car, adjusted the rearview mirror, and headed off to a lake in the Adirondacks, one of her favorite places on earth. It was there everyone was to gather and celebrate Vicki's life on a hot Sunday afternoon.

Road signs along the way told her life story.

Schenectady, where she grew up (and I spent college weekends eating pasta at her parents' table).

Albany, where her career in advertising flourished.

Saratoga Springs, where she lived.

Schroon Lake, where her family's cottage was a welcome summer refuge.

But it wasn't until I turned down a country lane that it hit me where I was heading, what was happening, why I was there. There, in a meadow, sat a large white tent filled with row upon row of white chairs.

As if on cue, college friends from Boston and Philadelphia began emerging from cars. There were hugs, tears, and the obligatory "It's great to see you, just not under these circumstances."

As for the service, I remember only bits and pieces.

There was a slide show of Vicki's life, the cast of characters so young and vibrant and optimistic, it was hard to believe it was ever us.

Simon and Garfunkel's "Bridge over Troubled Water" floated over the crowd, down the lane, and out onto the lake. It brought back memories of college dorms and smoke-filled rooms, a time when death meant Vietnam, not the Adirondacks.

Several friends spoke. People laughed. I managed a few words myself, sharing tales of a woman who loved air-conditioning, music you could dance to, and being a blonde, even if that wasn't God's intent.

And at the end, Vicki's best friend, a choreographer, danced on the makeshift stage with Vicki's daughter, herself a young and elegant dancer. They floated off down the aisle, out of the tent, onto the lawn, and into each other's arms.

Then it was over. A half century of life summed up in an hour. People lingered, chatting about how she would have loved it because, well, it was about her. And then we drifted away. Only memories lingered.

I drove back down the lane, the long, lonely shadows of a late-summer afternoon casting their melancholy spell.

The Sum of Our Summers

Remember when summer was summer?

When it really stood for something.

When every day was a holiday. Every outing an adventure. When a friend and a two-stick Popsicle were all that was needed to fill an August afternoon.

Life was an empty calendar, but never empty.

There were forts to build. Inner tubes to ride. Sprinklers to leap. Pup tents to pitch.

Summer spread out before us like a picnic blanket laden with goodies.

So much to sample.

So much time.

So what happened?

Now, here we are, midsummer and middle-aged, and it turns out summer is nothing more than just another season zipping by.

Summer? What summer? Jammed into a week's vacation somewhere along the way.

Summer's lazy, hazy, crazy days seem only hazy now.

Where did the lazy and crazy go?

When did the endless summer end? No one told us those magical nights of fireflies and lightning bugs would burn out.

Like most everything else, summer is wasted on youth.

I hated summer camp when I was a kid. Cried to come home.

Now I'd kill to return.

I'd weave those plastic boondoggles with the best of them.

I'd swim. I'd hike. I'd square-dance if that's what my counselor told me to do. I'd sit around the campfire, burn marshmallows on a stick, and sing my heart out.

Just the whole concept of someone sending me away for a free week in the mountains fascinates me now. Sounds like a lot more fun than waiting for a bus, whose air-conditioning hasn't worked since June, to take me to work.

Remember when air-conditioning was nothing more than riding fast on your bike?

When you never wore shoes?

When you got one haircut and it was good for all summer? You traveled light back then. Not even a comb. Not even a care.

Sunblock? What's sunblock? You tanned until you were as brown as a berry and you never worried about melanoma. Never heard of melanoma. Who's melanoma?

You didn't even have to worry about where your next drink was coming from then. Kool-Aid was served by the gallons in bright purple and green tin glasses, condensation dripping down the sides. Lime. Strawberry. Orange and grape.

Now it's iced tea in a paper cup. No sugar. On the run. Back to work.

There was no getting back to anything back when summer was summer. There was nothing to get back to. No Rolodex. No message light flashing.

You could just sit. Under a tree. On the stoop.

You hung out. For hours. For days. For weeks. For the summer. It all seems too good to be true now.

Whatever happened to those afternoons of slamming screen doors? To that world where Kool-Aid wishes and ice-cream dreams always seemed to come true?

You covered your world on foot back then. Or on your bike.

A summer storm never stranded you at LAX or O'Hare or La Guardia. If it rained, it was a bonus. A celebration. You rode your bike through the floods. Feet up.

You rode and rode and rode. Going everywhere. Going nowhere. The streamers on the handlebars fluttering in the wind.

If you did go in a car, it usually meant being transported from the good life to an even better one. As if you needed a vacation from the carefree life you were already living.

The beach. The mountains. Didn't matter. There was a swimming pool waiting. Or a dock on a lake. An amusement park. Miniature golf. A boat ride. Maybe just an ice-cream cone from the dairy bar a few miles down the road.

Your only problem back then was your brother—your brother who could turn the backseat into a war zone quicker than anyone.

So you yelled. And he yelled. Then your father turned around and yelled. You know now it's better to be the one yelling from the backseat than from the front.

Speaking of backseats, when was the last time you went to a drive-in movie on a hot August night?

See?

When was the last time you helped a turtle across the road? Or fooled around with a frog? A real frog. Not a bad date.

When was the last time you slept out on the lawn in a tent?

And speaking of tents, when was the last time you smelled

the inside of one, heated to perfection by an August sun? One of summer's better smells.

An all-inclusive vacation at a luxury resort has nothing on those summers.

The service was good. The food to your liking. Your hot dogs were grilled to perfection. Black.

The lemonade flowed.

And if you wanted to sell it instead of drink it, your entrepreneurship was rewarded. Just had to get out the old card table. Best thing was that every sale was 100 percent profit. No overhead costs. If only your business were set up that way today.

Was it all too much of a good thing?

Maybe. More than once you told your mom you were bored.

You'd ridden your bike a thousand miles and back, built your tree house, and vanquished all enemies from the front lawn.

Oh, to have the luxury of being that bored again.

Back when summer was still summer.

About the Author

CRAIG WILSON has been a feature writer for *USA Today* for eighteen years. In 1996 he began writing his very popular column, "The Final Word," which appears in *USA Today* every Wednesday. He grew up on a farm in upstate New York and now lives in Washington, D.C., with his partner, Jack, and their dog, Murphy.

About the Type

This book was set in Photina, a typeface designed by José Mendoza in 1971. It is a very elegant design with high legibility, and its close character fit has made it a popular choice for use in quality magazines and art gallery publications.